GIL STIEGLITZ

DEEP HAPPINESS:
The 8 Secrets

Deep Happiness: The 8 Secrets

© Gil Stieglitz 2014

Published by Principles to Live By, Roseville CA 95661
www.ptlb.com

Cover by John Chase

All Scripture verses are from the New American Standard Bible unless otherwise indicated.
New American Standard Bible: 1995 update.
1995 La Habra, CA: The Lockman Foundation.

ISBN 978-0-9838602-3-5
Christian Living

Printed in the United States of America

Dedication

This book is dedicated to my three daughters
Jenessa, Abbey, and Grace
and all the grandchildren
and great grandchildren
that will come through them.
You three have been one of the supreme delights of my life.
I can do no better than recommend to you and your children
to follow Jesus in the development of these blessed qualities.
Jesus was right; these qualities deliver the blessed life.

Table of Contents

Introduction

Have you ever looked up to the sky and cried out,

"Why did you let that happen, God?"

Of course you have!!! We all have. There are things that come slamming into our lives that are totally disruptive: a disease, a car accident, the death of a loved one, a pregnancy, a divorce, a governmental or business coup, or the loss of a job. In many cases we had nothing to do with this awful reality, but there it is in our lives. We want to shake the heavens and scream at God,

"Is this fair?"
"What is this for?"

I would like to suggest that there is another perspective about these uninvited problems. This book is not designed to be an explanation of all the reasons why God allows tragedy, problems, and injustice in the world. It sheds light on only one reason why God allows adversity, problems, and injustice into our lives. These realities of a sinful world are a way to move us toward a more excellent and blessed life. This book presents a radical perspective on the tragedies and problems of your life. God has not lost control and allowed evil to slip into your life unnoticed. Instead He has sent you hard tutors to teach lessons that need to become a permanent part of your life. I believe that He wants to use these things to bless you and help you build a great life. He sees a higher level of life available to you, and He is allowing this to give you the possibility of maximizing your life.

The Beatitudes are one of the answers to the question that is regularly on our minds,

"Why would God let this happen to me?"
"What is God up to in my life?"
"What is God trying to teach me?"

The answer in the Beatitudes is that God is enrolling you in self-improvement courses. Jesus tells us that the keys to a blessed life are having the eight qualities that we call the Beatitudes. The Apostle Paul says that we are the specific project of God (Ephesians 2:10). If this is true and if God loves us, then He is duty bound to try and teach us these qualities. He wants us to experience a blessed and successful life. The problem is that we don't want to learn these qualities.

What if God knew that in order to reach a new level of blessing in your life you had to develop a new level of gratefulness? Wouldn't He have to give you the opportunity to become grateful at this new level? You could reject the lesson. You could refuse to learn gratefulness at this new level and therefore miss the chance to have a new level of happiness in your life. But God – because of His deep love for you – He would continue to pursue you and give you more opportunities to develop this quality.

The problem with Jesus' teaching on the blessed life is that we don't want any of the qualities. Jesus says we must have them. Because we do not see the value of these qualities, we do not pursue them. We are too busy signing up for Power 101; Money 200; Respectable career 300; Beauty 300; Intelligence 400. None of these things are bad, but they will not produce the deep happiness that we are looking for – only the qualities that Jesus outlines will do that reconstruction project.

We see this pattern of God-directed self-improvement in the biblical characters over and over. Joseph was equipped to be a great leader and save a nation by experiencing slavery and false accusation and imprisonment. Moses was trained how to be a humble, patient leader by spending forty years tending sheep in the desert. David was taught how to be a great king by watching and being hunted by a mentally deranged king. It is often the adversity and tragedy that does more to shape great men and women of God than success and privilege.

Most of these courses are crucial to our reaching our fullest potential, but we resist learning these lessons. It is not that we don't want to reach our full potential; it is that we always think there must be an easier way. Surely God would not have to use affliction, tragedy, injustice, and oppression. While this remains theoretically true, God uses the circumstances of our life and even the evil of others to exercise us, develop us, and grow us. We do not know if there were easier ways for God to develop us if we had only chosen differently or if we had been in a different context. We do see the hundreds of examples of godly men and women who have all been trained by the "stuff" of life, and we must conclude that this is the way God has chosen to do it in our world.

When something happens to you and you do not understand, ask God this simple question,

"Which of the Beatitudes are you trying to develop in my life through this situation?"

"How is this designed to develop deep happiness and fulfillment in me?"

God will respond by pointing you to the quality(s) that this situation is designed to teach. I have found that when I ask these questions and go through the Beatitudes in my mind, God immediately brings to mind the quality He is working on in my present trial. The idea here is to cooperate with God, learn the lessons, and move forward on a great life. If you reject the lesson, then you move backward away from a blessed and truly successful life.

You do not need to pray for God to enroll you in these "success" or "deep happiness" courses. He loves you enough to inject these courses in your life whether you want them or not. On any given day we can discover that we have been signed up for a new level of personal development. The surface curriculum could be any number of things: a new boss; a cancer diagnosis, a layoff notice; a slanderous colleague; a car accident; a lawsuit; a rebellious child; an irritating neighbor. The list of possibilities is endless. God has surely allowed this adversity, crisis, or problem into your life for a number of reasons. (Now, let me say don't stay in a difficult situation if you can get out of it, righteously). But one of the reasons for difficult situations that is usually overlooked is because He wants to bless you by helping you develop one of the Beatitudes that you are lacking in some measure in your life.

God's job is to specifically design these "courses of instruction" so that we will get the maximum benefit from the training. It is our job to cooperate with God and develop the quality He is working on. If we do not cooperate and develop the particular quality, then God will only have to repeat the lesson. In many cases, if we don't learn the quality when He is trying to teach it, that opportunity will be lost. (You don't get to go back and marry your dream spouse from the past. You don't get to go back and get the job you missed because you weren't ready for the interview).

It is important to realize that these are courses of instruction and just like regular school there are quizzes, tests, projects, and finals. Why is that important to remember? Because if you do not do the work, develop the quality, and pass the final, the course repeats. I know some people who have been enrolled in humility class for decades. I have friends who will not learn to control their anger and they have totally diminished their potential. God keeps trying to teach them meekness and they won't learn it. They just let their thoughts, emotions, and power spray everywhere. What they do not see is that these displays cause people to pass them over for promotions, relationships, and increased influence. They sabotage their own blessed life. I wonder what would happen if our spouse, our boss, the interviewer were really honest about what they thought was keeping us from being successful.

Life is relationships. These eight qualities called the Beatitudes are the foundation under great relationships. There is fascinating research in the area of positive psychology which is reinforcing the power of Jesus' words. The researchers are telling us that the secular world has been looking at success all wrong. Our world has been telling us that we have to work hard to be successful because once we are successful (in other words: position, power, money, possessions, etc.), we will be happy. In other words, happiness is a moon that orbits the planet of success. But what the research is now telling us is that success actually orbits the planet called happiness. If we are truly happy (flourishing, content, loving, grateful, positive), then we will be successful. Their definition of happiness is very similar to Jesus' directions here in the Beatitudes. (*The Happiness Advantage*, Shawn Anchor, page 21)

The 8 secrets operating in your life right now

The following are three brief overviews and exercises using the Beatitudes as they actually operate in your life right now. They are either helping or sabotaging your life. If you cooperated with God's self-improvement program Then God is blessing your life. If you have been resistant to these qualities then you are right now undermining the success, blessing, and happiness you seek. Don't panic, if you find yourself in the negative list, just start cooperating with God on His current program in your life. In each of the three overviews of the Beatitudes circle areas God seems to highlight as you are reading through them. You may have more than one quality stand out as you move through them.

Exercise #1

In this first view of the Beatitudes, circle areas God seems to highlight. You may find a few stand out as areas of concern. God will be pointing out areas of needed improvement if you are willing to listen. Have fun and keep going. This is the beginning of a great adventure.

My life would be significantly happier and more successful if I…

1. were more grateful, teachable, and humble

2. processed my mistakes, wounds, pain, and losses

3. developed impulse control and used their emotions to fuel and enjoy life

4. pursued my dreams and righteous purposes with intensity

5. were forgiving, non-judgmental, and gracious

6. thought more positive, beneficial thoughts rejecting unethical, depressive, and selfish thoughts

7. savored each day, harmonized with the people around me and did not attack others

8. set boundaries for myself and others and was willing to sacrifice to protect those boundaries

Exercise #2

As you go through this second view of the Beatitudes, circle areas God seems to highlight as you are reading through them. You may find one or more stand out as areas of concern. In this list you will find that these actions and reactions are default settings for you. This would suggest that God and you have some work to do.

Right now, I am sabotaging the life I want because I am still...

1. self-focused, selfish, rebellious, and independent

2. covering my wounds and pain with silence, alcohol, drugs, pornography, sex, risk, etc

3. full of anger, rebellion, and impulsiveness and using my strengths for what I want in the moment

4. resistant to pursuing the dream God put in my heart and seeking pleasure without regard to who is damaged

5. harboring bitterness, judgmental, and plotting vengeance

6. filling my mind with sensuality, strife, vengeance, greed, and selfishness

7. fighting with everyone over everything and do not want to adapt to others

8. putting up with abuse done to me and at times abuse others to get my way

Exercise #3

As you go through this third view of the Beatitudes, circle areas God seems to highlight. You may find one or more stand out as areas of concern. In this list you will find God at work in your life in ways you may not have even noticed before. Cooperate with Him: pass the quizzes and tests.

Right now God is working in my life to...

1. be grateful, teachable, and humble

2. process my mistakes, wounds, pain, and losses

3. develop impulse control and use my emotions to fuel and enjoy life

4. pursue my dreams and righteous purposes with intensity

5. be forgiving, non-judgmental, and gracious

6. think positive, beneficial thoughts rejecting unethical, depressive, and selfish thoughts

7. savor each day, harmonize with the people around me and do not attack others

8. set boundaries for myself and others and be willing to sacrifice to protect those boundaries

The chart shows all these overviews of the Beatitudes as well as Jesus' original words. Some have used this chart as a placemat for the dinner table. Some have used this as a template to contemplate what God is doing while in the shower. Some have displayed this prominently in their bathroom or office so that they will see it every day. We know that the happiest people have developed one or all of these qualities.

The Beatitudes	The happiest people…	Explanation of the happiest people…
Blessed are the **Poor in Spirit** for theirs is the kingdom of heaven	**1. Are grateful, teachable, and humble**	Constantly grateful Teachable and correctable Humble and able to focus on others, not just themselves
Blessed are those who **Mourn** for they shall be comforted	**2. Have processed their mistakes, wounds, pain, and losses**	Take responsibility for their actions and words Grieve over their pain, wounds, and losses Grieve with others who have suffered great pain, wounds, and loss
Blessed are the **Meek** for they shall inherit the earth	**3. Have developed impulse control and use their emotions to fuel and enjoy life**	Have learned how to control their impulses Are able to convert their anger, emotions, and reactions into fuel for change Allow the wonder of their emotions to bring joy
Blessed are those who **hunger and thirst after righteousness** for they shall be satisfied	**4. Pursue their dreams and righteous purposes with intensity**	Pursuing their dreams, causes, and goals with intensity Know what is righteous and do not get involved with abuse Actively seek to right wrongs that resonate with them

The Beatitudes	The happiest people…	Explanation of the happiest people…
Blessed are the **merciful** for they shall receive mercy	**5. Are forgiving, non-judgmental and gracious**	Are forgiving not requiring that offenders receive the full measure of justice Are non-judgmental, making allowances for people's humanity and uniqueness Are gracious, giving people more than they deserve
Blessed are the **pure in heart** for they shall see God	**6. Think positive, beneficial thoughts rejecting unethical, depressive, and selfish thoughts**	Dwell in a positive, beneficial mental world Pursue constructive beneficial ideas rather than selfish, destructive, or harmful ideas Overwhelm fear, doubt, and obstacles with creativity
Blessed are the **peacemakers** for they shall be called the sons of God	**7. Savor each day, harmonize with the people around them, and do not attack others**	Harmonize and adapt within moral boundaries to their contexts Are peacemakers whenever possible Reject attacks, tension, and fear as a method of change
Blessed are those who have been **persecuted for righteousness** and for Christ… for theirs is the kingdom of heaven.	**8. Set boundaries for themselves and others and are willing to sacrifice to protect those boundaries**	Set boundaries for themselves – positive and negative Set boundaries for others – positive and negative Are willing to sacrifice to stop abuse and shed light on abuse

Secret #1

Poor in Spirit

MATTHEW 5:4
Blessed are the poor in spirit
for theirs is the kingdom of heaven

1
Poor in Spirit

Proverbs 11:2
When pride comes, then comes dishonor, But with the humble is wisdom.

When we are born we are helpless and dependent, but we are completely self-focused and selfish. One psychologist said if we were born full-grown we would rip our mother's head off for our milk. For babies, it is all about us. We bring joy to others as they hold, bathe, feed, diaper, and care for us. But we are about ourselves. If we are going to become deeply happy in this life (not just outwardly successful), we must learn how to lower our natural self-focus and raise our focus on God and others. We will still maintain a righteous self-interest, but the real treasures come in going beyond the early programming of selfishness. We will receive far more rewards, joys, and love from others than we can collect by greedily looking out for ourselves alone.

Unfortunately many people never escape this default setting in their life. They push their way through life only thinking about themselves and seeing every action in the world as to whether it helps or hurts them. It is even more tragic that some people have been taught that in order to be happy they have to be more selfish, not less selfish. Some declare that you must always go after what you want in every situation and with every person if you are to be happy. This is wrong. This is what the Bible calls foolishness – a focus completely on self that can lead to all kinds of personal and relational maladies. Solomon tells us that foolishness is bound up in the heart of a child, and it requires instruction and training for us to overcome this default selfish setting. In fact the book of Proverbs details sixty-six forms that foolishness can take in adult life and how those forms of self-focus destroy your maximum potential.

If we are going to become truly happy in the depth of our soul, we must go beyond selfishness and embrace the needs of others and the pursuit of God while retaining a righteous self-interest.

Jesus begins our instruction in the ways of deep happiness when He tells us that blessings come to those who are poor in spirit. This is so opposite of our normal self-focused programming. We must lower ourselves from the position of supremacy in our life if we are going to begin collecting the blessings that God has for us. In one sense Jesus does want us to focus on ourselves and adjust our perspective on the world around us in small but significant ways. It is like we are getting new contact lens, and we will see the world differently and that will reveal new opportunities to bless ourselves through blessing God and others. These exercises are serious work, but they will open up a new world that up until now your self-focus has obscured.

Jump into this series of exercises on developing a new attitude about yourself. As you try these exercises and watch the new people, opportunities, solutions, and joys stream into your life, you will see the world as not revolving around yourself.

Becoming Poor in Spirit - Humility

Jesus says that the person who is poor in spirit is a blessed person. The word "poor" is the word for abject poverty. It is a willingness to beg to receive what is needed. Jesus connects this word not to our social or financial status but to our understanding of the innermost core of our being, our spirit. He says that a willingness to acknowledge that your spirit by itself is not complete is a blessed quality. He is saying that the person who admits that he/she is not complete in and of themselves is brilliant and will be blessed. God said it to Adam in the Garden of Eden: "It is not good for man to be alone." We are incomplete creatures. We are needy creatures. We need God and we need others. We are blessed when we do not see ourselves as self-sufficient.

To see this truth from the reverse angle brings it into stark contrast. A cursed person is one who believes that they are self-sufficient in and of themselves. They don't think they need God, friends, family, co-workers, society, or anybody. The further you go down this road, the more cursed you become. This is a description of hell – alone, depending only on yourself, marooned, isolated, cut off from God's grace, separated from love, and refusing help. There are many who have chosen that path and God will ultimately let people stay on that path out into eternity – like wandering stars for which the black darkness is reserved.

This quality of poorness in spirit has at least six aspects, which together make up what Jesus calls poorness in spirit and most people call humility. It is not easy to develop this quality. It will require that we depend upon the grace of God because in many instances developing humility requires that we move in exactly the opposite direction than what feels right. However, the lack of this quality of poor in spirit holds thousands back from the success and joy that they want and God has planned for them. Begin today to open yourself to the power of dependence and a whole new world will open up to you. The following are the six ideas in this crucial quality of humility. Remember that God wants to bless you so He is regularly enrolling you in these courses so that you can be more blessed. To say it another way, some of the problems and challenges that you are facing will only be solved by the development of these aspects of the quality of humility.

1) Acknowledging our dependence on God and others

2) Becoming teachable: An openness to learn

3) Becoming God and others focused: Moving the spotlight

4) Becoming grateful: Unlocking the power of gratitude

5) Eliminating pride: Pulling in our plumage

6) Self-acceptance: Finding your place on the Team

First, the blessed person realizes that they are a dependent person. They need God and they need others. The more you are aware of this the more blessed you will be. The people who act as though they do not need anyone and have no room for God will not enjoy life. In order to have a great marriage it takes two people, not just one. In order to have a great career it takes lots of people, not just one person. In order to have a great family it takes all the members, not just one person. In order to be spiritually blessed it requires that you and God both cooperate to build a blessed life. The question in regards to this beatitude is whether we realize how we need God and the other people in our life.

Second, the blessed person has eyes to see lessons from everyone. The blessed person is teachable. Each person can teach us something. Everyone is the sum total of the choices they have made and what has happened to them. We can learn volumes from their choices and experiences. Did they make the right choice at certain key junctures in their life? Do they really understand all the consequences of their choices? What should they have done? How can they move forward from where they are? A good portion of humility is the willingness to be taught by God and by others. Many of the people that we bristle at are God's appointed instructors. Until we are willing to learn, we will just keep repeating the same destructive choices again and again. If something in your life is not working, then you have an area where you should be teachable. But I have watched lots of people who refuse to learn a new way in some aspect of their life (marriage, spirituality, finances, parenting, work, driving, etc) even though it is clear that their old way is not working. And in those areas where they refuse to learn, they remain stuck in a cursed loop. Don't let this be you. Become teachable.

Third, the blessed person is focused on others and not themselves. The person who is poor in spirit is impressed with others and acknowledges who the other person is and how much they have going for them. Too often humility has been described as thinking of ourselves in the worst possible terms and trying to lower our estimate of ourselves. This is not humility but destructive thinking. This is the wrong way to go about it. Raise your estimate of others. Focus on how wonderful, talented, and capable the other person is; and you will be closer to viewing reality about yourself. Yes, there are times when we must make sure that we have a realistic estimate of ourselves and deflate any overblown thoughts about ourselves, but one of the best ways to do this is to focus on and trumpet the good qualities of others.

Humility is being God and others centered. We can acknowledge our gifts and contributions and even find great joy in them, but we must more importantly be able to continue to lift others up above our own estimate of ourselves. (Philippians 2:1-3) Find the area(s) where the other person is better than you and focus your attention there. Find the place where the other person is in need and help them. True humility takes into account who we are on both the positive and negative side but chooses to focus on others, their good points, and their needs. False humility leaves the focus on yourself, whether that it your good points or your bad points. True humility pushes the focus onto others even while you know that you have great worth.

Fourth, the blessed person is a grateful person. It is not possible to be truly humble without gratefulness. There is nothing that we have that we did not receive. Often, we act as though we have earned and/or deserve some or all of our blessings. The more that the cancerous attitude of "I deserve this" spreads, it kills God's ability to bless you with great treasures. If you are not willing to develop gratefulness for what you already have, then why should He give you more? Becoming grateful is like an antibiotic to our souls that kills the toxins of apathy, superiority, arrogance, and prejudice. It is a shame when God must enroll us in a gratefulness class because we won't learn it any other way. If God must strip everything away from us to teach us gratefulness, He will, because gratefulness is more important than all the stuff we think we deserve and need. Remember the cursed person is the ungrateful person.

Fifth, a truly blessed person has stopped trying to impress people with showy displays, trivial accomplishments, and overbearing attitudes of superiority. The truly blessed person has turned off the "let's focus on me" machine. The humble person is looking to make a positive contribution even if no one notices. I call this aspect of humility "pulling in the plumage" because we often act like peacocks spreading out our accomplishments, degrees, clothes, cars, salaries, and other cultural babbles in order to impress people and gain some type of superiority over them. As long as we are still playing the game of puffing ourselves out to gain an advantage over others, God will not bless us. We have to get past this form of life and live lives of substance and real impact.

Sixth, a truly blessed person has come to terms with who they are and who they will never be. They are poor in spirit in that they realize that they have a significant contribution to make, but they also realize that they are not capable of doing everything. I am dependent on who God made to be. God has built into your life many unchangeable features: your parents, heritage, height, early years, mental and physical abilities, and capacities. Many of these you may want to change but you cannot. Accept yourself rather than rail against God who did this to you. Do not be a bad imitation of someone else. It is important that you become a full version of yourself. Accept who you are and agree to cooperate with God on being the maximum version of you. We will never be truly able to experience life if we continue to reject who and what we are. Yes, there are some aspects of our past that we may need to overcome, but even those things require an admittance of their reality in order to move towards neutralizing its impact.

I have watched numerous very talented young men throw away their talents, years, and gifting because they will not develop this quality of humility or poorness of spirit. Let me introduce you to one such person who was one of the most gifted, intellectual, and high potential people I have ever

26

known. Let's call him Jim. The more I got to know him, the more impressed I was with all the abilities that God had given him. Everyone who knew him was just waiting for God to use Jim in huge ways. But it never happened. He had all kinds of opportunities, but the blessings and results never materialized. In fact, the ministries he did become involved in decreased in size and impact over time. Ultimately he never realized his full potential. Jim lived in a world where it was terribly important for others to recognize how smart he was and how fortunate God was to have Jim on His side. Jim was constantly focused on himself. Even when he was trying to help others, it became a way to show how smart, generous, Christian, and loving he was. I watched as God enrolled Jim in "courses" in humility, but the lessons were never learned. God will pass over the self-focused person and elevate the less skilled person who is poor in spirit. One of the most difficult lessons to learn is that the world does not revolve around you or need you. God would love to use you, but He does not need you. Your lack of involvement is not a block to Him; it is only your loss.

The bad part of pride is an excessive self-focus. This bad part of pride is the opposite of poor in spirit. If you are to receive the blessing of this Beatitude you must know how to focus on God and on the other person. Humility is not the negation of your talents, gifts, abilities, and presence; but it is a desire that the focus be on others or God and not yourself. There will be times when people want to acknowledge your abilities and presence and that is fine, but the humble person does not need to have that spotlight. The humble person accepts what is true about themselves, their impact, and hard work; but they quickly deflect the attention from themselves and on to others or to God.

27

I have been in the position of evaluating and hiring people for much of my adult life, and I can say that one of the major things that holds people back from greater ministry impact is arrogance: "Did you notice how wonderful I am?" "I'm superior to you attitude." "I'm really better than this job." "Aren't you impressed with me?"

This negative form of pride is an excessive self-focus whether that comes out as arrogance or hypochondria. Whenever you will not allow someone else to be the focus of attention, you are proud. An excessive self-focus will destroy our potential and our relationships. This sin is the beginning of Satan's ways (Isaiah 14:12) and is the beginning of movement away from wisdom and righteousness. God has asked each of His servants to walk in humility. When we develop pride we shut down valuable people, lessons, and opportunities that Gad has for us. We must examine all the ways where the cancer of pride has spread through our lives and move toward the powerful position of living in humility.

Exercise #1

Ask God which of the aspects of humility – poorness in spirit – He is wanting to develop in your life. Remember you can't work on all of these at the same time. A little improvement goes a long way to increasing a blessed life. Cooperate with God in these aspects of humility and watch His blessings come.

1) Acknowledged dependence on God and others

2) Becoming teachable: An openness to learn

3) Becoming God and others focused: Moving the spotlight

4) Becoming grateful: Unlocking the power of gratitude

5) Eliminating pride – Pulling in our plumage

6) Self-acceptance: Finding your place on the Team

Acknowledged Dependence
on God and Others

Philippians 2:3
Do nothing from selfishness or empty conceit, but with humility of mind regard one another as more important than yourselves

We have been told that the rebel wins; that the loner is the real hero; that the independent person who doesn't need anyone else is the measure of success. Think about how many movies tell the story of the hero as the rebel who goes his own way, who pushes away at all help, and who stands against the majority to prove them wrong. This is completely wrong. It is the opposite of what Jesus is saying in this key phrase about how life works. It is the person who understands how they need God and others that allows them to have a blessed life.

Only when we develop a realization of our dependence on God and others will we experience the full blessing of being poor in spirit. Salvation is the realization that we constantly need God in our life and that we also need the other people He has allowed into our lives. It is very helpful to remind ourselves of how much we need God. Answering the question "what am I counting on God for today?" can give a fairly accurate measure of our love for God.

Let me give a little balance here as some people have become so dependent on others that they have become paralyzed about making choices. The kind of dependence that Jesus is trying to promote is a healthy interdependence not an oppressive dependence built from fear.

Exercise #1

Let's look at a few exercises here to heighten our awareness of our need for God and others in our life. It is only as we learn to acknowledge that we need God and the others that He has placed in our life that some of our arrogant self-sufficiency will be knocked down. This is a crucial exercise.

I regularly take out a blank sheet of paper and try and write down all the ways that I need God at that time, during that day, and in that week. If I cannot write down fifteen ways that I need God for that week in 60 seconds, I know that I have allowed myself to become lukewarm in my love for Jesus.

Exercise #2
DEPENDENCE ON GOD

What do I need God for? We need to be able to consciously examine the ways we are depending on God or our love for Him will grow cold, and we will unconsciously slide toward the world's way of living. Answer the following questions which will show you whether you are dependent upon God in your everyday life.

1. What do I need God to do in my relationship with Him?

2. What do I need God to do in my marriage?

3. What do I need God to with my family?

4. What do I need God to do at my work?

5. What do I need God to do in my finances?

6. What do I need God to do with my friends?

Exercise #3

DEPENDENCE ON OTHERS

All of us must come to realize that we are not self-sufficient, but that we really need the other people and institutions in our life. It is only our willful disregard of these people and institutions that allows us to believe we are self-sufficient. Many people do not come to realize how much they need their spouse until they are gone. Many people do not understand how valuable their government is until they are in another country that does not play by the same rules. Most people have been gripped by loneliness that they were not expecting when they went on a trip without friends or family. We are social creatures, and its only pride that suggests that we do not define and validate ourselves by the relationships that we have. Only when we consciously acknowledge our need of others will humility become a permanent resident in our life.

Answer the following question for the people in your life.
Come up with at least five items each.

In what areas or ways do I need my...

Spouse

Family

Work

Friends

Community/City/State/Nation

Becoming Teachable
Learning from everyone and everything

Philippians 4:12
I know how to get along with humble means, and I also know how to live in prosperity; in any and every circumstance I have learned the secret of being filled and going hungry, both of having abundance and suffering need.

Ephesians 4:1-3
Therefore I, the prisoner of the Lord, implore you to walk in a manner worthy of the calling with which you have been called, with all humility and gentleness, with patience, showing tolerance for one another in love, being diligent to preserve the unity of the Spirit in the bond of peace.

One of the quickest ways to limit your future is to not be teachable. Have you ever watched a person who is new to a job but acts like they know more than those who have been there for years? It's a huge turn-off, isn't it? If we are going to be truly blessed, we must develop this aspect of poor in spirit: teach-ability. Do others perceive that we are teachable, correctable? All of us have blind spots and areas where we can learn new things. If the people around us perceive that we won't listen to the insights and information that they have, they will not share these things. They will watch us fail and stumble even though they have what we need. People are always willing to help a person who is willing to learn.

Each person can teach us something. We all can learn from everyone. Everyone is the sum total of the choices they have made and what has happened to them. You can learn from their choices. Did they make the right choice at certain key junctures in their life? Did they make a really bad choice? Why was it a bad choice? Do they really understand all the

34

consequences of their choice? How can you avoid making the kind of bad choices that they made? How can you make the kind of good choices they made?

God is trying to teach us to learn lessons from all kinds of people and all kinds of situations. One of my mentors wanted me to understand that God would often put me in situations where my bosses, my colleagues, my neighbors, and even my family would say what was offensive or nonsensical to me; but that I should look for the truth in what they were saying. I did not necessarily have the right to dismiss what they were saying immediately just because it was different. I can remember one professor I had in college who hated everything about Christianity and everything about me because I espoused Christ so frequently. She took great delight in pointing out my flaws and mistakes. My mentor at the time refused to allow me to dismiss what this professor was saying. He wanted me to be teachable. He made me dig for the truths in what she was saying. He required that I look for how God might be teaching me through her invectives. This was a different type of learning than I had been involved in before. It changed my approach to life. Even though this professor hated Jesus and did not in any way want to further my work for God, she did. I was able to see God at work in and through her and I got better at writing and thinking because of her. God does not waste experiences. God puts people in our lives for reasons. Yes, if the person is immoral or unethical and we can get away from them, then we should; but we must become teachable at a whole new level.

I had the privilege of watching Dr. Francis Schaeffer work a room before and after his lectures. He seemed drawn to the person who was different – the person who did not fit in. He was not threatened by them but intrigued. He knew that they were who they were because of the choices and influences on their life. He wanted to listen to them. He wanted to hear their story. He wanted to learn. He did want to share Jesus with them, but he was all about the learning first. This is what made him different and very effective. He was always teachable and always learning, even when most of us thought he had all the answers.

Exercise # 1

If we were to ask key people in your life, would they say you are teachable or that you tend to resist correction?

Spouse: Teachable / Resist Correction
What would you need to do to demonstrate you are teachable to this person?

Family: Teachable / Resist Correction
What would you need to do to demonstrate you are teachable to this person?

Boss: Teachable / Resist Correction
What would you need to do to demonstrate you are teachable to this person?

Colleagues at work: Teachable / Resist Correction
What would you need to do to demonstrate you are teachable to this person?

Subordinates at work: Teachable / Resist Correction
What would you need to do to demonstrate you are teachable
to this person?

Friends: Teachable / Resist Correction
What would you need to do to demonstrate you are teachable
to this person?

Exercise #2

What would the most significant people in your life
have you learn from them? There is a wealth of specific
knowledge all around you about how to improve your life and
career and yet we so seldom ask. The people who are closest to
us really do know what is holding us back from reaching our
dreams. Ask them!!!! Ask them to tell you one area or one
blind spot that they think is limiting you from reaching your
full potential.

Spouse:
What is one thing that your spouse thinks is a blind spot or is
limiting you from reaching your full potential?

Family:
What is one thing that your family thinks is a blind spot or is
limiting you from reaching your full potential?

Boss:

What is one thing that your boss thinks is a blind spot or is limiting you from reaching your full potential?

Colleagues at work:

What is one thing that your colleagues at work think is a blind spot or is limiting you from reaching your full potential?

Subordinates at work:

What is one thing that your subordinates at work think is a blind spot or is limiting you from reaching your full potential?

Friends:

What is one thing that your friends think is a blind spot or is limiting you from reaching your full potential?

Exercise # 3

This is for those who want to get the maximum benefit out of developing a teachable attitude. It is an advanced exercise which may be difficult for some and for a few who are in oppressive situations, it may be unwise.

Ask significant people in your life who love you and care for you to write down the answers to four questions. This may only be one to four people in your life. You may want to hand them a copy of this page of the book so that they can see it and have a sheet to respond back.

What should I stop doing?

What should I keep doing?

What should I start doing?

What should I do more of?

When they have responded back to you, write them a thank you note for their candor and encouragement. Remember all the information that you need to live a blessed life is all around you residing in the people you already know. You have to get it out of them. Be willing to receive it and sift through it making the appropriate changes with God's grace.

Exercise #4

List each person in the following group and write what you can learn from watching them or seeking instruction from them or what they can teach you. If you have never asked them for any advice, ask them. It will be very instructive and entertaining.

Family

Relatives

Friends

People at work

Church

Neighborhood

Becoming Others Focused
Moving the spotlight

Philippians 2:4
Do not merely look out for your own personal interests, but also for the interests of others.

Too often humility has been described as thinking of ourselves in the worst possible terms. This is not humility but destructive thinking. Yes, we are sinners who have no hope of heaven without the sacrifice of Christ, but we are His treasure and He invested the death of His Son in our redemption. God sees us as valuable. Humility is being God and others centered, lifting our opinion of others up above our opinion of ourselves. You can have a very high opinion of yourself; just have a higher opinion of others (Philippians 2:1-3). Realize that the other person has hopes, dreams, talents, and gifts just like you do. They hope that someone else will be interested in them and their abilities. They will find it easier to love you if you will regularly focus on the things that are strengths for them. Find the area(s) where the other person is better than you and focus your attention there.

My life changed dramatically when I started to make this change in how I was around others. There was a time (it lasted way too long) when I was always trying to impress people with who I was, what I knew, and the things I have done or could do. I found that when I put the focus on the other person and began trying to learn about what their dreams were and what their skills and achievements had been, just by listening I blessed them and developed a friendship. Often I learned incredible things that I would never have been exposed to if I had continued my, "Let me tell you how wonderful I am crusade."

41

Let me tell you about the man who is the living embodiment of this quality. His name is Dr. Mick Boersma. He was a mentor of mine and gave me a chance to teach classes at the university where I studied (I will be forever grateful for that opportunity). He had this interesting ability to never let a conversation be focused on himself. You would find yourself going on and on about yourself and your deepest secrets because of his questions and his focused interest in you. He would ask you questions about you, your family, your interests, your dreams. At some point in every conversation I asked him a question about his family and his desires. Just to be polite. Sometimes I would apologize for talking so much about myself. But very quickly he would have me back talking about myself with him eagerly listening. The whole process fascinated me so much that I began to study him to figure out how he did it. It became a contest with me. Could I find out more about Mick than he found out about me? Could I demonstrate how much he meant to me by the questions I asked and the way I listened? How long could I keep Mick Boersma talking about himself rather than my talking about myself? He is this amazing man with amazing accomplishments and a truly remarkable wife and family, but I had to discipline myself to not let his wonderfully inviting questions about myself derail me from asking a better question about him and what he was learning, doing, and enjoying. After numerous failures in the school of Boersma, I eventually, after years of attempts, could hold my own and demonstrate to him the insatiable curiosity and great questions that he always had for me. He was probably the best at personal relational skills I have ever met. And it all revolved around his intense others-focus. He is enjoying deep happiness because of a full attainment of this quality.

One of the things that humble people do is that they regularly move the spotlight off themselves and onto God or

42

others. This begins in their mind. All of us have a natural tendency to focus on our own ideas, our desires, our needs, but one of the key ingredients of true humility is to shift that spotlight on to God and what He wants, what He would be pleased with, and what He thinks about the situation in front of you. The other thing that truly humble people do is they ask questions about the other person. Most people will answer sincere questions about themselves. Just shift the focus from yourself to others or God and your humility will go way up. This frees God up to bless you more because He knows you will not use the blessing to become even more self-focused.

Too often people, in trying to be humble, spend all of their time trying to lower their estimate of themselves. This is the wrong way to go about it. Raise your estimate of others. Focus on how wonderful, talented, and capable the other person is. Yes, there are times when we must make sure that we have a realistic estimate of ourselves and deflate any overblown thoughts about ourselves, but one of the best ways to do this is to focus on and trumpet the good qualities of others.

True humility chooses to focus on others, their good points, and their needs even while you know that you have great worth. False humility leaves the focus on yourself whether that is your good points or your bad points.

Exercise # 1

How can I focus on the other person? The key seems to be genuinely curious about others through a steady stream of questions. What are they thinking? What they are dreaming? What they are feeling? What do they want to talk about? The key to an others-focus is to ask questions. Ask questions that they would like to talk about. Too often we wait for someone else to ask us questions about what we want to talk about.

Exercise # 2

Can you focus on what the other person needs and on their good points instead of always needing to be centered on your needs, desires, and wants?

Who are the people God has put in your life?

Spouse, friends, co-workers, bosses, civic leaders, family members, spiritual leaders, neighbors, service people you see regularly.

What do they want to talk about?

What are their good qualities and skills?

It can be so easy to notice one or two irritating traits or actions in these people and miss the wonderful things about the person. Don't let that happen to you.

Becoming Grateful
Unlocking the tremendous power in gratitude

Ephesians 5:20
always giving thanks for all things in the name of our Lord
Jesus Christ to God, even the Father

A number of years ago, I made a decision to go from noticing all the things that were wrong around me to noticing all the things that were going right around me. What an incredible difference? I had been negative, critical, and increasing cynical. But when I stopped trying to correct every fault, every flaw, every mistake, and instead started noticing and commenting on every sincere effort, every good deed, and every correct answer it was like God just turned the lights on in my life. Everything changed. People wanted to hang around me. My mood went from dark to upbeat. I began to see all kinds of good things that could happen in the future instead of all the things that could go wrong. There are still things that go wrong and huge mistakes that the people around me make, but we overcome those because our focus is not on the mistake but on the good stuff. Becoming grateful is a choice. Yes, some people notice more of the things that are not right, but if they were to turn their observation powers to the positive side they could notice more good things. We receive from the Lord more of what we are looking for. If you are looking for the negative you will get more negative. If you start noticing and looking for positive, then you will get more good and positive. This is just the way that life works. Try it – you will like it.

The blessed person is a grateful person. It is not possible to be truly humble without gratefulness. There is nothing that we have that we did not receive. Often we act as though we have earned and/or deserve some or all of our

45

blessings. The more that the cancerous attitude of "I deserve this" spreads, it kills God's ability to bless you with great treasures. If you are not willing to develop gratefulness for what you already have, then why should He give you more? Becoming grateful is like an antibiotic to our souls that kills the toxins of apathy, superiority, arrogance, and prejudice. It is a shame when God must enroll us in gratefulness class because we won't learn it any other way. If God must strip everything away from us to teach us gratefulness, He will, because gratefulness is more important than all the stuff we think we deserve and need. Remember the cursed person is the ungrateful person.

One of the things that many churches try and do for their teenagers is to take them to another country into its poorer regions or another city into its poor regions to open the eyes of the young adults to the blessings and benefits that they enjoy. In most cases this is a traumatic event and causes a new level of gratitude for a few weeks. Then eventually the young person re-acclimatizes to their surroundings and begins to take their normal amenities for granted. The question for youth pastors and parents is how do I cause the attitude of gratitude to be more permanently injected into these young people? Realize that God is trying to do the same thing with all of us. He knows, as you know, that an attitude of gratitude will allow you to be more successful, more blessed, more full of joy, and less cynical and doubtful. Realize that God is injecting situations, circumstances, and people into your life so that you will become more grateful for what you already have. Learn the lesson and start noticing all the good things already in your life. The more you notice what you already have the more God can give you. The less you notice of the blessings you have already received, the less He can send.

Exercise #1

Daily Gratitude

In this exercise we are seeking to orient you to all the positive and encouraging things going in your life. Every day this week write down three good things that happened to you that day. This forces you to look for the good that God is flowing into your life every day. It will cause you to start seeing more of it. God is blessing you every day in all kinds of ways that you are missing because you are not looking for it. Take time at the dinner table or staff meetings or over in a meeting to let people know what the three positives were that day.

1.

2.

3.

If you focus on telling people three good things about your life every day for a month, it will change your orientation and your ability to see the good all around you.

Exercise #2
Journal of Gratefulness

One of the best ways to think through those people who have helped you become what you are is to think through your life chronologically. This journal is designed to cause you to put specific events in their proper context, to give thanks to the people who have helped you, and to mention their unique contribution. Many times you will find that certain people are mentioned more than once. This is to be expected. They need to be thanked more than once. A heart full of gratefulness is a heart open to God's lessons and grace. Take each age grouping and think through the people who helped you in that time frame. Be specific with how they helped you. Make an effort to thank these people through a letter, a phone call, a note, face to face, etc., but develop a gratefulness perspective. "What do you have that you have not received?" "And if you have received it, why do you act like you had not received it?" You may have to ask others about much of what took place between birth through age five.

0-5

6-10

11-15

16-20

21-25

26-30

31-35

36-40

41-45

46-50

51-55

56-60

61-65

66-70

71-75

76-80

Eliminating PRIDE
Pulling in Your Plumage

1 Peter 5:5,6
... all of you, clothe yourselves with humility toward one another, for GOD IS OPPOSED TO THE PROUD, BUT GIVES GRACE TO THE HUMBLE. Therefore humble yourselves under the mighty hand of God, that He may exalt you at the proper time.

The street I live on has been adopted by a flock of wild turkeys. This means that on any given morning you might find a gaggle of turkeys on your roof or your front lawn. It is quite funny to watch this big group of odd-looking birds wander through the neighborhood just out of reach of the dogs, cats, and people. One of the things their presence means is that in the spring during mating season we get to watch the males puff themselves up to their maximum size, spray out their hind feathers vertically, and yell, "gobble, gobble, gobble" to impress the various women turkeys in the group. The bigger the male turkeys can make themselves appear, the more women they can collect in their harem. This puffing out of the turkeys is the perfect picture of us being proud. When we do this: we wear our most impressive clothing; we drop every famous name we know; we use every big word we have ever heard of; we mention all of our degrees, experiences, skills and abilities. All with the intent to show that we are very important. All of us have the ability to inflate our importance well beyond our actual significance. This is the opposite of being poor in spirit. When the Bible speaks of being humble, it often means to pull in one's plumage.

A truly blessed person has stopped trying to impress people with showy displays, trivial accomplishments, and overbearing attitudes of superiority. The truly blessed person has turned off the "let's focus on me" machine. The humble person is looking to make a positive contribution even if no one notices. This aspect of humility is pulling in the plumage because we often act like peacocks spreading out our accomplishments, degrees, clothes, cars, salaries, and other cultural babbles in order to impress people and gain some type of superiority over them. (Yes, I know that in certain situations, occupations, and contexts you must have plumage to even have a conversation; but you don't have to always be showing it.) As long as we are still playing the game of puffing ourselves out to gain an advantage over others, God will not bless us. We have to get past this form of life and live lives of substance and real impact.

Just a note of balance. Some have taken this idea of humility being pulling in your plumage to mean that you should not have any plumage or strive to attain any credibility in the world's eyes. This is not the case. Humility is about not showing our plumage just to focus on ourselves. There are times to display plumage because these are the entrance tickets for the people you are dealing with. There are times to talk about your degrees, your accomplishments, and your titles. There is plumage that you absolutely must strive to obtain if you are going to serve those whom God is calling you to serve. The peacock doesn't always have to walk around with their feathers out. But God did not strip the peacock of the feathers to make him humble. The peacock is just supposed to show them at the proper time. Gain the degrees. Go to the right school. Buy the right car. Dress fashionably. But do not become all about the plumage and be ready to pull it in most of the time so that others and you can realize that you are just a normal person saved by grace.

The opposite of poor in spirit is being arrogant, haughty, bigoted, pre-judicial, and/or dismissive. When a peacock is trying to show off, it puffs itself up and shows all of its plumage and aims all of its importance and beauty in a particular direction. Humility means pulling in your plumage and just being yourself. Yes, you can puff yourself up with all of the important people you have met, all the important titles and awards you have won, and all the brilliant thoughts you have thought and words you know. But is that really necessary? When we believe we are so superior to another person for any reason (gender, race, background, mental abilities, handicap, financial status, marital status, appearance, etc.), we cut ourselves off from God's instruction through that person. We then cut ourselves off from the wisdom of God and the will of God by the degree of our arrogance. Only when we recognize, confess, and repent of our arrogance will we be open to the fullness of God's instruction and blessing.

Years ago a friend of mine worked as a deputy sheriff in the county jail. He said that he remembers one young man who came into the jail who was still trying to walk, talk, act, shrug, and gesture with all his gang posture. The deputies made it clear to the young man that that kind of behavior and attitude would not be permitted in the jail. They made him practice walking, talking, pointing, and standing normally. As they enforced those conditions, it stripped all the bravado and inflated superiority out of the young man; and he was just a scared young man named Jay. It was at that point that Jay became able to learn a new way of living. He was not able or willing to learn as long as his arrogant posturing was still a part of his persona. God says that to us. I can't get through to you when you are trying to still be this puffed-up person. Bring the sails in, pull the plumage in, just be a regular person, and live life a different way. It really is a better way.

All of us have plumage which we think makes us look more important. It could be the way we dress, the car we drive, the degrees after our name, the way we walk, the salary we earn, the title we have, the parents or ancestry we have, the people we know, and a thousand other things. God asks that we be ready to pull that plumage in and just be our regular plain vanilla self, energized by Him. He says that learning to live a life of love and trusting Him without all the posturing and plumage will pay off with a more blessed life. The Apostle Paul says that God asked Him to lay aside all of those things that we gain or pride-producing for him and just be a follower of Jesus. Paul was willing to do that in order to know Christ at a deeper level. Paul tells us in Philippians that God does not require everyone to lay aside every piece of plumage in their life like he had to do, but we must be ready to do it if Christ demands that.

Exercise # 1

When you want to impress people with who you are, what do you have a tendency to emphasize or do?

What would pulling in your plumage look like in your life? Describe yourself being loving, helpful, kind, and joyful without trying to get people to notice you or being impressed with you.

Exercise #2

Make a list of the individuals and/or groups that God has placed in your life whom you have puffed yourself out towards or acted as though they were inferior to you. Please also list the way you expressed your arrogance or superiority. Finally, add the way you think God would want you to express your new-found humility and acceptance.

	Who	What	Expression
Example	Sally	Ignore, stare	Apology, hug, invite to party
Family			
Friends			
Neighbors			

	Who	What	Expression
Example	Sally	Ignore, stare	Apology, hug, invite to party
Colleagues			
School			
Church			

Acceptance of Self
Finding my place on the team

Psalms 139:13-15
For You formed my inward parts; You wove me in my mother's womb. I will give thanks to You, for I am fearfully and wonderfully made; Wonderful are Your works, And my soul knows it very well. My frame was not hidden from You, When I was made in secret, And skillfully wrought in the depths of the earth.

When I was in high school I discovered three things about myself that didn't seem to help in my desire to be popular or successful after high school: I had strong athletic legs; I was drawn to spiritual activities; and in spite of my introversion, I like to talk in front of groups. I tried to embrace all of these things individually, but it didn't amount to much. I went out for the cross-country team and made the team but near the back of the pack. I started attending our church more, hoping to find God in a deeper way, but it was largely dead. I wanted to connect with God, but I couldn't make contact through my church. I enjoyed speaking up in class and giving oral reports but joining the debate team held no interest at all. There were times when I tried to will myself to being a better runner, a more spiritual person, and/or a better oral presenter; but it didn't amount to much in the end. Eventually our church hired a new youth pastor who helped me put it all together. He helped me see that I was not a jumble of individual talents, but that God had something in mind when He gave me these gifts and talents. I was not meant for me to be an athletic superstar or just a church attender or a salesman. God had given me all of these things to combine them and have me become a pastor, professor, and teacher. As long as I stay in this stream of activities, I feel His pleasure.

A truly blessed person has come to terms with who they are and who they will never be. They are poor in spirit in that they realize that they have a significant contribution to make, but they also realize that they are not capable of doing everything. I am dependent on who God made me to be. God has built into your life many unchangeable features: your parents, heritage, height, early years, mental and physical abilities, and capacities. Many of these you may want to change but you cannot. Accept yourself rather than rail against God who did this to you and be a bad imitation of someone else. It is important that you become a full version of yourself. Accept who you are and agree to cooperate with God on being the maximum version of you. We will never be truly able to experience life if we continue to reject who and what we are. Yes, there are some aspects of our past that we may need to overcome, but even those things require an admittance of their reality in order to move towards neutralizing its impact.

Exercise # 1

What are your positive unchangeable features? Have you thanked God for each of these?

Spiritually

Heritage

Mentally

Emotionally

Physically

What are your negative unchangeable features? Have you thanked God for each of these?

Spiritually

Heritage

Mentally

Emotionally

Physically

What are your spiritual gifts?

What are you passionate about?

What are your abilities and talents?

What is your temperament and basic personality?

What experiences have happened to you to shape you?

Exercise # 2

We are dependent upon who God made us to be. Many are trying to deny who God made them to be or run from who they are, but that is not the path of blessing or peace. We are dependent upon our body, soul, and spirit in this world to help define us and show us the way to our purpose. The unique combination of our unchangeable features is a huge part of the puzzle of who we are supposed to be.

How have you tried to deny a talent, gift, or ability that God has given you?

What would you need to do to start using that talent, gift, passion, or ability again?

We do not get to choose who we are. We are the unique combination of the gifts, talents, and abilities that God wove into our being. If we have no talent for singing, no amount of singing lessons will turn us into a singer. If we have no empathy, no amount of counseling training will turn us into a great counselor. One of the things that holds people back from the blessed life is that they are trying to be something or someone that they can never be. Blessing and joy are in the path of accepting who God made you to be and going down that path.

Pray a prayer of acceptance of your unchangeable features. It important to let God know that you have come to a place of acceptance about the body that He has slipped your soul into. One day He will remove your soul from its current body and put it into another one with lots more features. But until that day we need to let Him know that we accept the body He has given us, and we will do all we can to maximize it for His glory.

Dear Heavenly Father,

I come in the name of the Lord Jesus Christ and bow before you in worship and praise. I want to thank you how you have made me, physically, emotionally, mentally, and spiritually. I realize and admit that I have not always been willing to embrace or enjoy who I was. I confess that that is not the path to peace and joy. You have made me special with unique talents and gifts. You knew what you were doing when who I was to become was knit together in my mother's womb. You do not make junk and I am not junk. You have a purpose for my life. I want to cooperate with you and fulfill my purpose. Show me the way to use more of your grace and mercy. Thank you especially for _____ which is an unchangeable part of who I am that I have rejected in the past.

In the Name of the Lord Jesus Christ,
Amen

Secret #2

Mourning

MATTHEW 5:5
Blessed are those who mourn
for they shall be comforted

2
Mourning

Mourning Your Own Sin
Mourning the Sin, Injustice, Oppression in the World

It is almost un-American to allow yourself to grieve or feel pain. We would rather take a pill than feel pain. We want to get past grief as soon as possible. It is really strange that Jesus says that the ability to grieve and process pain is absolutely essential to live in this world with a deep happiness.

Jesus is saying something profound on a number of levels with this second Beatitude. He is saying that there will be injustice, oppression, sin, and evil in our world; and we must have a strategy to prepare for it and a way to work through it. It is amazing that the God of the universe tells us how to work through the injustice and sin in the world He created rather than ending it. He has said He will end it but that is the next life, not this one.

The Beatitudes are not just nice platitudes for middle-class people who don't have to experience the real world. No, Jesus tells us how it really is and what we will need to have to experience deep happiness. We will be treated unfairly. We will have people sin against us. We will see and experience injustice that we cannot correct. What should happen doesn't always happen.

We need to be ready to process the sin that will enter our lives. Some of it will come from ourselves and some of it will come from others. When Jesus says that we need to be prepared to mourn, He is implicitly saying that you will sin and others will sin against you. If we are to be deeply happy and not destroyed by these betrayals, we will need to process our pain.

I have two friends who have advanced degrees in Alcohol and Chemical Dependencies. Both of these men were addicted to alcohol, heroin, cocaine, and a number of other substances. They know that world inside and out. They are clean and sober now. They both told me that there are only two things that are true of real addicts. One, they have found a substance or activity that dulls the pains in their life. Two, they have a wound that they are hiding or hiding from that they have not processed that keeps needing to be medicated. If a person will not started processing the pain in their live, they cannot be helped because they haven't touched the reason for the addiction.

I have had the privilege of walking with a number of people through their deep search inside of themselves. This is a painful walk through the wounds, sin, mistakes, evil, and destruction but a necessary one if we are going to experience the blessing that Jesus talks about in mourning. If we want to experience deep happiness, we cannot refuse to take a deep look at ourselves and what has happened to us. This is not a quick journey in many cases, but it is a rewarded one. Find a safe person who will walk with you through the process of mourning and you will see new blessings begin to emerge in your life.

Mourning Your Own Sin
Developing a Clear Conscience

People who move to the depths of Christian spirituality have learned to mourn. They mourn over their sins, over their pain, over their losses, over the pain they have caused others, and over the pain and loss in the world. The Western World ignores this Beatitude. In order to receive the blessings of mourning, we must do it much more deeply than most want to go. It begins with the process of developing a clear conscience which is essential for a servant of Christ (1 Timothy 1:18-20). Without a clear conscience one cannot be sensitive to the Holy Spirit as He guides us through life.

Developing a clear conscience. 1 Tim. 1:18-20; Luke 17:3

A clear conscience means that we have made every attempt to apologize, make right, and repair damage that we have done to others. The Scriptures tells us that as far as it depends on us, we have made peace with everyone whom we have wronged (Romans 12:18). We want to continue the process of developing a forgiving heart by developing a clear conscience which is essential for a servant of Christ (1 Timothy 1:18-20). Without a clear conscience, one cannot be sensitive to the Holy Spirit as He guides us through life. One of the key places that we sense the Holy Spirit is in our conscience. When our conscience is clean without offense before God or man that we know of, we are able to understand and respond to the Holy Spirit better.

Have you ever watched someone make the same mistake over and over again? Usually we cannot see ourselves making the mistake; we can only see that we are getting the same bad results.

We are still lonely.
We still have a lousy marriage.
We are still poor.
We are still angry.
We still don't know God in any meaningful way.
At the end of each month we run out of money.
A disagreement with our spouse ends in yelling
   and screaming.
We get passed over for a promotion again.
We keep getting fatter.
We didn't get the date we wanted.
The house is still a mess.
We have no new friends.
We are no closer to our dream house than five years ago.
We are still disappointed.
We are still depressed.
We are still out of shape.

All of the above are results that should tell us that we are making the same mistake over and over again. But too often we keep doing the same things and expecting a different result. We will never get a different result until we acknowledge that we have made bad choices in the past, and then we can start making new ones in the future. It is essential that we do what Jesus tells us in order to become blessed with a different life. We need to mourn the bad results we are getting, looking for the choices that we are making that are producing them.

God wants you to maximize your life (Ephesians 2:10). He wants you to be experiencing the best that is possible for your life for His glory. I realize that sometimes circumstances, governments, family, or other factors keep you from doing all you could do. But most of the time the problem in your life is you. Even if the problems are not your fault, it is you who are going to have to do something to keep those other things from derailing your future.

Spend time asking God where you have made bad, harmful, and/or destructive choices. Assume that all the bad results of your life are somehow in your control. What could you have done differently? (I am not suggesting that you get into a depressive cycle of blaming yourself for all the problems in your life. I am suggesting that you take an honest look at where you need to make different choices by owning what you have done in the past.) What choices could have been different? What should I do in the future? Apologize and try and make amends for the harm you have done.

There is a long and illustrious tradition in Christianity of serious Christians mourning their sins and the pain they have caused. From the confessions of St Augustine to the ruminations of Theresa of Avila there is a need for personal mourning over one's own selfishness. Don't shy away from this process but embrace it. Realize that there is often some action, words, attitudes that could have been different on your part that caused much of what you are experiencing. When you realize that it was you who had some part in this situation, then you free yourself from having to repeat the same problem.

David in Psalm 51 says, *Search me and try me and see if there be any wicked way in me.* If we are to be more than surface Christians we must allow God to break us with the ways that we have wounded others.

Let me give you two spiritual exercises to get this process started.

Exercise #1

Pray a prayer of confession: As you are going to bed at night, ask God to point out ways that you have been sabotaging His work in your life. Ask God about each of the seven deadly sins and let Him speak to you. The seven deadly sins are: Pride, Envy, Anger, Lust, Sloth, Gluttony, and Greed. Pause after each one of the sins and see if God brings you back to time during the day when you were guilty of these. Don't invent times of sin. Just let God bring conviction if you are guilty. Then ask for His forgiveness that is in the life, death, and resurrection of Jesus Christ. Thank Him that it is available. Ask Him to show you how to not commit those same sins tomorrow. You will hear God speak to you in the depth of your spirit, seeking to bring conviction and then healing to your life. He does not convict in order to condemn, but He convicts in order to gain confession so He can apply forgiveness and healing. Do this every night for at least seven days.

Here is a sample of how the prayer time might go:

Dear Lord,

Have I committed any pride? (Pause and let God speak to your heart and bring any arrogance, superiority, bigotry, or prejudice to your mind. If He does, then agree with God that it was wrong and ask that the forgiveness that is in the death of Christ be applied to that sin. 1 John 1:9)

Then move on and ask, *Dear Lord, have I committed any envy?* (Pause and let God speak to your heart and bring any jealousy, envy, and/or depression over the blessings of others to your mind. If He does, then agree with God that it was wrong and ask that the forgiveness that is in the death of Christ be applied to that sin. 1 John 1:9)

Then move on and ask, *Dear Lord, have I committed any anger?* (Pause and let God speak to your heart and bring any anger, violence, bitterness to your mind. If He does, then agree with God that it was wrong and ask that the forgiveness that is in the death of Christ be applied to that sin. 1 John 1:9)

Then move on and ask, *Dear Lord, have I committed any lust?* (Pause and let God speak to your heart and bring any immorality, sensuality, and/or inappropriate sexuality to your mind. If He does, then agree with God that it was wrong and ask that the forgiveness that is in the death of Christ be applied to that sin. 1 John 1:9)

Then move on and ask, *Dear Lord, have I committed any sloth?* (Pause and let God speak to your heart and bring any procrastination, laziness, and dereliction of duty to your mind. If He does, then agree with God that it was wrong and ask that the forgiveness that is in the death of Christ be applied to that sin. 1 John 1:9)

Then move on and ask, *Dear Lord, have I committed any gluttony?* (Pause and let God speak to your heart and bring any overeating, drunkenness, or repetitive behaviors that are addictive to your mind. If He does, then agree with God that it was wrong and ask that the forgiveness that is in the death of Christ be applied to that sin. 1 John 1:9)

Then move on and ask, *Dear Lord, have I committed any greed?* (Pause and let God speak to your heart and bring any stealing, scheming to defraud or manipulate another for personal gain to your mind. If He does, then agree with God that it was wrong and ask that the forgiveness that is in the death of Christ be applied to that sin. 1 John 1:9)

Thank God for the forgiveness that is yours in Jesus Christ if you will trust Him to be your Savior. If you have never prayed any prayers of dependence upon Christ, then get started with a prayer like this:

Dear Jesus,

I admit to You that I have been and continue to be selfish. I recognize that I have violated your standards of how life was supposed to be lived. I do want a relationship with You, God. I want to thank you for dying on the cross to pay the penalty of my sins. I want you to be the boss and guide of my life. Come into my life and make me the kind of person you want me to be.

In Name of the Lord Jesus Christ,
Amen

Exercise #2

There is something powerful about admitting where you sinned against God, made mistakes, bad judgments, and/or harmed someone else. Sometimes what you are blaming yourself for is not really your fault after all. Sometimes what you are hiding from needs to be owned as your fault so you can move on and put this issue behind you.

How to clear your conscience. Luke 17:3

Write out a list of those whom you have deeply wronged.

1.

2.

3.

4.

5.

6.

7.

8.

9.

10.

Write out a list of all those who were once close but are now distant.

Indicate the potential reason for the distance.

1.

2.

3.

4.

5.

6.

7.

8.

9.

10.

Contact the people you have wronged and seek to understand (education) in what ways you might have offended them.

People will help you understand how you offended them if they are convinced that you really want to change and not commit that type of offense again. If we are to be sincere disciples of Christ, then we must be committed to growth and movement toward Christlikeness.

First you must seek rebuke (Luke 17:3). In other words, you must ask others to educate you on how you offended them. This means asking them to tell you and preparing yourself to not defend yourself if they do tell you.

You must be gentle in spirit (Proverbs 15:1). You can never expect that people will really help you understand how you have offended them if your spirit voice and facial expression does not say that you are humble and ready to learn. They must really sense that you want to know. This means, on your part, you must see the relationship as more important than your pride, your way, and your ease. It will be difficult to hear your offense from their point of view, but it is essential if you are to learn and they are to release the offense and heal the distance.

They will toss out a few safe offenses to see if you are listening before they give you the real one. It is often true that people will see if you are listening by telling of some small offenses that may or may not relate to the real offense. If they see that you are really seeking to understand and change, they will share the larger offense with you.

Do not defend yourself or try and clarify any misunderstandings at this point. You must take a non-defensive posture in these times. It is best to approach them as though you were a recorder writing down a list of grievances about someone else other than yourself. If you do have an explanation for why a particular thing happened, save the explanation until after they are finished and they realize that you came to listen.

Relive your offense through their eyes.

You must feel the offense from their point of view. Often having them tell you the offense from their point of view is enough. At other times you must spend time reflecting on how much your offense would have hurt if you had been in their place. You can relate it to a similar experience in your life if that helps. They must know that you realize how offensive your actions were.

Do not let yourself reduce the importance of your offense by repeating what they did first. When you look at what you did, do not rationalize that you were forced to do it because... Realize that you had a choice and you did what you did. Take responsibility for it. You may have to list out the options that you could have done in response to their actions or the actions that preceded your doing what you did.

1.

2.

3.

4.

5

6

7

8

9

10.

Agree with them concerning your offense (confession). Luke 17:3

Realize that they see your offense as bigger they you do. Ask yourself how big they see your offense in terms of causing the distance between you and them. ___%. The offense that they are holding against you may seem insignificant to you, but it is not to them.

Tell them you were wrong for what you did. State clearly without any excuses that you realize that you were wrong for what you did. Do not imply or say that they were wrong also. Do not say, "If I was wrong, please forgive me." Admit you were wrong,

Clarify what took place, if a genuine misunderstanding has taken place, but only in a spirit of humility and gentleness. Always give them the benefit of the doubt. If you believe that there was a misunderstanding or they are just not aware of something that would change their minds, it is most helpful to share it in this fashion: "I may be mistaken, but I think that there are a few things you may not be aware of that will explain why I did what I did. May I explain?"

Remember the goal here is to come to a mutual understanding of what happened and the part you are responsible for. Confession is agreeing with the other person regarding a situation. Remember the goal is to have everyone agreeing at the end. This can mean agreeing that you were wrong.

If the offense is serious or has occurred regularly and involves a continuing relationship, share your repentance plan (repentance). Luke 17:3

74

One of the most difficult and common bitterness and clear-conscience problems is the problem of repeated offenses. If you admit that you were wrong and do not want to commit the offense again but you repeatedly offend someone, your apology will not seem valid. This is when a repentance plan comes in. We often need some punishments or consequences that can be administered by the one we are offending to remind us to not keep doing this. We should come up with a number of ways that the person we have offended can administer the reminder. If we both have chosen, then we will not forget very often. What are the possible repentance plans or punishments for each offense that could be administered to you to help you remember?

1.

2.

3.

4.

5.

6.

7.

8.

9.

10.

This may mean or involve restitution. Repentance also involves restitution if the offense involved the destruction, stealing, or incapacitation of real property or money. Your repentance plan may include paying back twice* what the item was worth.

Ask them to forgive you (forgiveness). Luke 17:3

Pose the question, "Will you forgive me?" Wait for a response. You need to hear them say yes. They may need time to see if you are genuinely serious about your desire to change and stop offending them. Let them have the time. Forgiveness is not something you can demand because you followed a few prearranged steps. It is rather a privilege granted by the offended party, after we have admitted guilt and asked for pardon.

If they choose not to forgive you, then you may have to start again on the education step with an even gentler spirit or work on the repentance plan (sometimes you need to let them have a part in developing the repentance plan). Often they do not think you mean it, that you will not really change, or that you do not really understand how much it hurt.

It is possible that they will not forgive you because of their own hard hearts, or what it would mean they would have to do, or because then they would have to ask forgiveness of you. If that is the case, then you have sought to be at peace with all men as far as it depends on you.

Mourning
Your Losses, Your Wounds, Your Pain

Another important element in receiving the blessing that Jesus promises in this Beatitude is in mourning your losses, wounds, and pain, We remind ourselves that it is the next world that is perfect, not this one. We live in a sinful, broken world that will hurt us and disappoint us. We must have a way of processing the pain that will surely come our way. The therapy that Jesus tells us we must have is mourning, grieving, and processing our pain. God created this world with real choice and real destruction that can come from our choices. This is not a Disneyland world where everything is fake. Choices will echo through generations. So be careful what you choose. Galatians 6:7 "Do not be deceived, God is not mocked, Whatsoever a man sows that shall he also reap."

Let me briefly remind us that God has asked us to be managers of this world (Genesis 1:26). He has asked us to build our marriages, run our governments and raise our families and treat each other with love and righteousness. He wants us to be involved in the development of this world in which we live. Many wonder why God did not develop a perfectly complete, perfect world and drop us into it. But that would be a world without choice. Injustice is a fact that grows from our choices and incomplete understanding of how much God has put us in charge. He has told us what to do but given us the ability to reject His advice. God has given this world and all its inhabitants the ability to choose to love Him or to choose to reject Him. The majority of the world has chosen to stay self-focused, living themselves on the throne of their lives.

For many of us the sin of others is deeply damaging and long lasting. What happened to us at the hands of others was evil. Jesus says that in order to survive in this sinful world we must be ready, willing, and able to grieve many of the things that have happened to us and will happen to us. It is very powerful to process your pain by getting it out of your soul through writing, talking, and even praying it out.

We live in a sinful world in which terrible things happen to us because other people are allowed to make selfish choices. These losses, wounds, and pain can cripple us if we do not process them. To mourn means to process these significant negative events in our life. It could be the death of a loved one. It could be a sexual molestation or rape. It could be a divorce. It could be abandonment or loneliness. It could be the loss of a job.

Jesus was right when he said that we cannot be truly blessed in this sinful world without practicing mourning. Remember even He mourned the physical death of Lazarus in John 11.

I have two friends who each wasted over twenty years of their lives in alcohol and drug addictions. Both of them have been delivered from that slavery and have gone on to advanced degrees and now are helping people who are lost in the same addictions they struggled with. They both told me that there are essentially two things that make an addict. One, you must be in the presence of the substance that is addictive to you. Two, you must have a wound that you are trying to self-medicate so you don't have to feel its pain any more. Both of these men separately told me that when they try and help an addict, they must help the person bring out the wound or all treatment will fail. It is the unprocessed wound that keeps them addicted to whatever will make that pain go away.

This is why Jesus' statements in this Beatitude are so prescient. We must know how to mourn to survive this sinful world. There will be pain, wounds, and loss as we live out our lives. We must be able to process the difficulties of those times if we are going to enjoy a blessed life.

Exercise #1

Write down in a journal or take a walk by yourself and tell God about the painful things that have happened to you.

Exercise #2

You also may want to write a letter to your oppressor (that you will not send) expressing all that you feel about what they did, said, or planned to do to you. We know that this was Abraham Lincoln's favorite way to process the pain he went through. After his death, his secretary found a number of unsent unopened letters to his generals that expressed his true feelings about their faults and mistakes during the Civil War.

Exercise #3

Make an appointment with a counselor, a trusted friend, a pastor, and/or a safe person and talk through some or all of the most painful episodes in your life. This may take time.

Exercise #4

Pressing Even Deeper

In deciding to be honest about our life, we must answer the following questions if we are to get a handle on what may be in the way of a joyful life. It is entirely possible that the following questions may need to be answered numerous times as new pain, wounds, and losses are remembered.

1) What traumas, losses, wounds, difficulties, and hurts have I suffered through and how might they be affecting my life?

2) What is your family's way of dealing with these kinds of problems and issues?

3) What is your current culture (friends, community, media, authorities) directing you to do, say, and think about the issues and problems of life?

4) What actions have you taken and/or words have you used that you are deeply ashamed of and wish that you could take back?

Secret #3

Meekness

Matthew 5:5
Blessed are the meek for they shall inherit the earth

3
Meekness

Blessed Are the Meek –
Their Strength Is Under Control

Developing Meekness

To be meek means to have our strength under control. If a person has little or no impulse control they will not enjoy life. They will always be reacting to their environment. The higher they rise and the more God blesses them, the more they need to be able to feel their reaction inside but not necessarily let any part of it out until they have figured out a constructive way to do that. In order to be truly successful, a person must have their strengths under control.

Meekness involves adapting to God-given authority and discerning when our rights, privileges, possessions, and even our schedule are in the way of God's plan. The easiest way to begin discovering this violation is by looking at your anger and desire for rebellion. Sometimes our anger and/or rebellion is a signal that God is seeking to do something different with our lives than what we had planned at that moment.

There are few things more pathetic than a talented, intelligent, and/or gifted person who cannot direct their abilities in a controlled way. The person who has a great voice must be able to sing the right notes at the right time or their talent will be wasted. The person who can run fast is not a great football player unless they can run the right play, wait for their blocks, and fake people out at the right time. The person who can tell a great story only becomes a great speaker if they fit the story into a great speech and can tell it at the right time and leave out all the details that will make it too long. In order to be truly great in every part of life, we must have our strengths under control. We must have our strengths working properly in the right systems.

Life is basically a series of systems. A system is just a repeating pattern of actions that you do in certain situations. How and when you shower or bathe is a system. How you greet people for the first time is a system. What you do when you are disappointed is a system. How you react when you don't get your own way is a system. Your strengths are at the mercy of your systems. If you have great strengths but bad systems, you are significantly handicapped. Everyone has strengths, abilities, desires, and passions that need to be successfully applied to life. In order to be truly successful at life you must be willing to learn new systems. This requires flexibility and adaptability which are key components of meekness. When we get angry, it is usually a breakdown of one of our systems. Anger is often the opposite of meekness. Anger is usually a signal that we want something to change, but we don't know how to bring about the change in the right way. External anger is raw energy for change, but it is leaking out or being forced out of the system we are using.

All of us have systems to do almost everything. A system is a step-by-step series of actions for dealing with assignments, problems, chores, and issues. If you have done something three times in a certain way, it has most likely become your system. Our systems become our life. Some people call these their routines or habits. We have systems to get up in the morning. We have systems to get dressed. We have systems to handle depression. We have systems to deal with our finances. We have systems for enjoying the weekend. We have systems for exercise. We have systems for eating. We have systems to handle disagreements. We have systems for celebrations. We have systems to deal with loneliness. We have systems to deal with boredom. We have systems to deal with physical pain, and we have systems to deal with soul pain.

Where do our systems come from? Many of our systems we learned from our parents. Some we picked up from friends. Some came from schooling. Some we invented on our own. Some of our systems are really helpful. Some of our systems are destructive. Some of our systems hold us back. Some of our systems were helpful in one context, but they are inappropriate or damaging in another. Some of our systems feel helpful, but they are deeply destructive to our future and/or to those around us.

Most of us are required to have multiple sets of systems for the various roles or situations we live in. We may have a different set of systems for work or school than we do at home or with family. We may have a different set of systems for dealing with bosses than when we are dealing with peers or when we are dealing with subordinates. While we may have multiple sets of systems for various contexts, situations, and roles, they should share a common moral framework or mental and moral gymnastics will also become destructive.

We can usually discover our systems by asking the question: "What do I do when I am facing this situation, this kind of person, or this problem?" And then write down the things we do step by step. What many of us will discover if we write down our system is that we have really defective systems in a few places. We may also discover that we have no system for some problems.

Exercises in System Thinking

1. What do you usually do when you get depressed?

2. When you want to have a "good time," what three things come to mind?

3. How do you respond when you don't get your way?

4. What do you do when you start feeling lonely?

5. If someone is mad at you, screaming, or yelling, what do you do?

6. When you feel attracted to another person romantically, what do you do?

7. When you have the chance to make a lot of money, what do you do?

8. Right after an argument, what do you usually do?

9. If someone has manipulated you, what do you feel like doing?

10. Who or what is the most important person or thing in your life?

11. When you don't know what to do – What do you do? Who do you ask?

12. What do you do when you run out of money?

13. What are three ways you earn money or have earned money?

14. When I want to be respected, I do this?

15. What do you do when you like someone?

16. How would you let a person know that you are grateful to them?

Some of us have a good system for dealing with friends but a lousy system for dealing with authority figures. Some of us have great systems for dealing with bosses, parents, and superiors but completely inadequate systems for making and keeping friends. Some people have great systems for making money but terrible systems for managing or saving money. Some have great systems for being successful at school but inadequate systems for work success. Some have great systems for impressing people or making friends but lousy systems for being by themselves. There are systems for all of these issues and situations. They will be different than what you have been doing, and at first they will not feel "right" but keep practicing them. Pour your strength into this new system and you will get the new results you are looking for.

What I want you to realize is that in most cases if a person is successful at something (making friends, getting promotions, getting good grades, saving money, or being slim), it is not because they are more gifted than everybody else; it is because they have a successful system. If you learned and did their system, you could have their success. Yes, some successes only come because of talent or abilities, but even those with talent and abilities must have the right system.

It is our systems that leave us stuck where we are. It is our systems that sabotage our future. If we have a bad system for dealing with depression that relies on alcohol or illegal drugs rather than friends, counselors and new behaviors, we will remain stuck or cycle into destructive behaviors. Are you willing to become adaptable and flexible to learn new systems so that you can have a new life?

Let me give you an example I see all too often. A young man or woman is traumatized by something in their elementary years or teen years (a rape, parent or friend die, molestation, a divorce, a break-up, a betrayal). They have incredible soul pain which they do not know how to handle. (Someone should tell them how to mourn as Jesus said in the last chapter). They don't know how to talk about what they feel. They don't know who to talk to and the people they try to talk to are not safe or won't listen. They take a drink of alcohol or smoke a joint or snort a drug, and the pain in their soul is gone as long as they are drunk or high. They try a few other things to get rid of the pain in their soul and yet nothing does as complete of a job as the drug, the alcohol, or the joint, so they keep coming back to this "solution." After three to ten times it becomes their system for dealing with soul pain. They do not know that this is a destructive system that will rob their future and destroy the intimacy with others that they really want and need. They do not know that this "solution" will force them to steal, cheat, lie, and hurt those they love the most. They do not know that alcohol, drugs, and porn will draw other problems and friends who will keep them stuck in a life going nowhere.

We can learn new systems. We are not stuck doing life the way we have always done it. If there is a better way to do something, we can learn it. All of this has to do with meekness. Meekness is strength under control – the willingness to be flexible and adaptable in living our life. We cannot be successful in life if we are not flexible and adaptable. We cannot be successful if our strength is not under control. We may have, in the past, punched people or yelled and screamed in rage to express our strength. We can learn a new system and bring about change.

It is the systems that we must examine, and it is our systems that must change.

Rebellion

One of the overlooked sins of the Western culture is rebellion. God has established a number of authorities in our life to keep us from getting into trouble and to keep us from inventing the rules for our own benefit. He first places in our lives parents and then as we grow up, we are given governmental authorities, spiritual authority, marital authority, and even vocational authorities. It is these authorities that put a frame around the pictures of our lives. God has placed them in our lives for our good. As long as those authorities do not ask us to do immorality or evil, we should find a way to work with their authority.

The life of the rebel is hard. When rebellion is for selfish purposes, it yields a bitter fruit. One of the consistent sins of teenagers in America is the sin of rebellion. They try and develop their own independence through direct rebellion against their parents, teachers, or church officials. The impulses of rebellion are let out and their life takes a radically different turn. Some find their way back from these rebellious ways but many ingrain a disagreement with authority. Later when the person wonders why they don't get hired or why they never get promoted, they don't realize that they are giving off an "I am not a team player."

In 1 Samuel 15:23 Samuel the prophet tells Saul that rebellion from the clear direction of God is the same as practicing witchcraft. Both of these sins expose the person to the direct power and influence of Satan, the enemy of our souls. The rebellious person believes that they are making up their own mind but once they directly rebel from a moral order from a God-given authority, they are impacted by strong spiritual influences.

Our culture keeps suggesting with movies, books, articles, and the heroes our culture promotes that the independent rebel is the one who wins, but it isn't true. Think through all the heroes in our popular culture and notice how often it is the rebel who screams at parents, lies to bosses, openly disagrees with governmental authorities that is celebrated. Yes, when one thinks differently to solve a known problem that is applauded, but that is not being a rebel. When one perseveres in accomplishing their dream in spite of setbacks and difficulties, they are not a rebel; they are persistent and perseverant.

There are times to rebel when an authority is seeking to make you violate God's laws or forcing you to be immoral. But those times are not prevalent in our present day. Don't choose the life of the rebel. It sounds alluring and exciting, but it is not keeping your strengths under control. Rebellion is most of the time letting your selfishness demand its way over those who really have your best interests at heart.

One of the tricks that the Devil uses to move us far from the will of God is to get us to rebel from our God-given authorities over issues of personal preference and/or ego. These "I got to be me" rebellions sound good in the movies but almost always end up badly. If the Devil can get you to believe that your rebellion is noble and heroic, he can keep you far from the will of God. Being a part of God's team means not being a lone wolf who invents the rules as he goes.

Two examples of rebellion

Let me talk about two forms of rebellion that saps the joy from our life but does not seem like rebellion. First, if you have any leadership abilities, people will begin to come to you with complaints and criticisms of the organization and deposit their issues and problems at your feet. There is a temptation to pick up these complaints and begin leading a charge to right these wrongs. If you are not careful you can become the leader of the complainers, the leader of the wronged. You are the one with the guts to speak up against the leader, the teacher, the pastor, the system. If you are not careful, you become the leader of the opposition. In many cases you don't care about these issues personally, you just want to lead something. This is a way to waste your life. Don't use your leadership for other people's complaints. Unless their complaints rise to the level of morality or criminality, don't be seduced into this form of rebellion. No organization likes this internal rebel. You will be passed over for promotion and marked out as a malcontent. If you go down this road, you will often find yourself wasting your mental, emotional, physical, and spiritual energy trying to right problems that those people need to solve on their own.

The second form of rebellion is a cynical rebellion. If you are observant or you are not at the top of the organization, you will notice problems in the organization. You will be tempted to keep track of the wrongs you suffer and tell others. This will lead you to the other cynics and negative people. If you are not careful you will find great camaraderie in being negative, cynical, and pointing out that the organization has problems. This is a waste of your life. This is rebellion. Right the wrongs and be positive. Keep your negative, critical, and cynical impulses under control.

Exercise #1

If we were to ask your God-given authorities, would they say that you were adaptable and amenable to their direction or that you were resistant, rebellious, or stubborn? Be willing to take a long look at how rebellious you really are. You may also ask them what they would say to the above question.

- o   God:

- o   Parents: If still living at home

- o   Government:

- o   Spiritual Leaders:

- o   Employer:

- o   Spouse:

Exercise #2

Look at the God-given authorities in your life. Are you right now resisting or fighting them over a non-essential issue? Yes, there are essential issues where rebellion is called for but that should be over violating one of God's standards or immorality.

- ○ God:

- ○ Parents: If still living at home

- ○ Government:

- ○ Spiritual Leaders:

- ○ Employer:

- ○ Spouse:

Exercise #3

If you were to let your God-given authorities know that you would fully cooperate with their wishes (unless it involved evil or immorality), what would be different in your life? Name three things that would change if you were to fully cooperate with their wishes.

- o God:
  1.
  2.
  3.

- o Parents: If still living at home
  1.
  2.
  3.

- o Government:
  1.
  2.
  3.

- o Spiritual Leaders:
  1.
  2.
  3.

- o Employer:
  1.
  2.
  3.

- o Spouse:
  1.
  2.
  3.

Anger
Ephesians 4:22-27

Anger is a form of selfishness and protection. It most often results when we do not get our own way or are hurt. It is usually an adult temper tantrum. God has stated clearly that if you are going to get angry, then your anger should last no longer than a day. (Ephesians 4:26-27)

Most of the time our anger is because we have an unrealistic expectation about something. We expected something to turn out perfectly for our benefit. And when it didn't happen the way we expected, we are angry or frustrated. Many times our anger is a signal that we have developed an unrealistic expectation about a person or situation. The situation or person may need to change, but it was unrealistic to expect that it would be our way given the level of communication, planning, or previous practice.

Definition of Anger

Anger is a warning sign to our soul. Anger indicates that there is some right, expectation, possession, or fear that is not realistic to our current situation.

Anger is energy which wants to bring about a change. If this energy is harnessed and used for righteous purposes, it can be quite productive. If this energy is allowed to explode out without proper boundaries and direction it will wound and destroy. If this energy is used for selfish purposes alone, then it will also cause great damage.

Types of Anger

The Scriptures describe the following eight types of destructive energy that flow from us when we do not get our way. Most people have a "favorite" two or three that they use to vent their frustration.

Anger: Emotional explosions brought on at the lowest levels by selfishness, hurt, or fear

Rage: Sustained external anger of an uncontrolled intensity

Wrath: Fierce anger, indignation, strong sustained rage

Outbursts of Anger: Explosive, impulsive, external anger

Burning Resentment: Hanging on to anger that was felt in the past. Holding a grudge against someone who wronged you.

Seething: Deep, internal loathing

Malice: Internal ill feelings toward another which may go so far as to plan or wish revenge, evil, or misfortune to other persons or ourselves

Strife: Anger that has broken into the open and resulted in open hostilities

Exercise #1

Who and/or what regularly brings out anger in your life?

1.
2.
3.
4.
5.
6.
7.
8.
9.
10.

Write the reason you were angry.

Write down what kind of anger did you experience or express. Please refer to the above list.

Under each episode of anger above write something God might be wanting you to yield, understand, change, or overcome.

Note: In order to yield, overcome, or understand you must believe that God has plans other than just taking something away from you. Sometimes He may be trying to develop something in you and can only accomplish it by asking you to yield, overcome, or understand. Other times He is trying to do something for others.

Exercise #2

Say the Lord's Prayer multiple times (potentially 5-10) before speaking.

Slow your breathing down and quote a verse of Scripture under your breath as you breathe in and out.

James 1:19
Let everyone be slow to speak, slow to anger and quick to listen.

James 1:20
The anger of man does not achieve the righteousness of God.

Ephesians 4:31
Let all bitterness and wrath and anger and clamor and slander be put away from you, along with all malice.

Psalms 46:10
Be still and know that I am God.

1 Corinthians 13: 4-6
Love is patient, love is kind and is not jealous; love does not brag and is not arrogant, does not act unbecomingly; it does not seek its own, is not provoked, does not take into account a wrong suffered, does not rejoice in unrighteousness, but rejoices with the truth;

Exercise #3

The 5 Questions: One of the most helpful exercises for dealing with repeating anger is to ask and answer five questions about the situation. Anger is a usually a response to an unmet or unrealistic expectation. You have to uncover that expectation and do something with it if you are going to change your reaction. Take your time answering these questions.

What were you hoping (thinking, expecting) would happen?

What went wrong?

What could you have done instead?

What can be done so that problem will not arise?

What system will you put in place to make sure you act differently before that type of situation?

Let's take a deeper look at where your systems may have come from. It can be very helpful to examine where our routines and systems come from. They have been operating behind the scenes for years, controlling our behavior and attitudes. When we bring these up and examine them, people are always amazed that they have been unconsciously operating on some bad information.

Personal and Family History

One of the most significant things people can do is to grasp how much of their actions and reactions to life have come from their parents. In many cases we are unconsciously acting just like our parents. In order to be meek we must develop new systems for controlling our strengths and our impulses. This involves examining the ones we now have. Most people learned the majority of their habits, systems, and ways of handling life from their parents or guardians. This next section helps you look at the habits and systems that your parents or guardians taught you that you may be unaware of.

1. Money

How did your parents handle money?
1.

2.

3.

What were your parents' sayings and attitudes toward money?

1.

2.

3.

What did your parents model in regards to making, managing, or giving money?

1.

2.

3.

Did your parents teach you anything about making, managing, or giving money?

1.

2.

3.

In what ways are you handling money the same way that your parents did?

1.

2.

3.

2. Success

What did your parents say or believe made a successful life?
1.

2.

3.

What messages did your parents give you about success in life?
1.

2.

3.

How did your parents try to become successful?
1.

2.

3.

What was your parent's success plan?
1.

2.

3.

3. Feelings

How did your family deal with feelings and/or expressed emotions; i.e. crying, shouting, screaming, anger, hatred, etc.?

1.

2.

3.

What did your parents say about people who expressed their feelings or emotions?

1.

2.

3.

How do you handle feelings? Is it like your parents?

1.

2.

3.

4. Roles of Men and Women

How did your parents model the roles for men and women?
1.

2.

3.

How would you like your mate to act?
1.

2.

3.

How close does your ideal mate conform to the actions of your parents?
1.

2.

3.

What did your parents model about how a man should behave?
1.

2.

3.

What did your parents model about how a woman should behave?

1.

2.

3.

5. Physical Affection

How physically affectionate were your parents?

1.

2.

3.

Did they say anything about public displays of affection?

1.

2.

3.

6. Compliments and Praise

When would you receive compliments or praise from your parents?

1.

2.

3.

What did your parents model to you about compliments or praise?
1.

2.

3.

What was the greatest compliment or praise you ever received from your parents?
1.

2.

3.

What do you believe is God's way of handling this area?
1.

2.

3.

7. Sexual Relations

How did your parents deal with sexual relations?
1.

2.

3.

What did they say or do to teach you about sexual relations?
1.

2.

3.

8. Loss and Grief

How did your family handle grief and significant loss?
1.

2.

3.

What did your parents say or teach you during times of significant loss?
1.

2.

3.

How long did your parents allow themselves or you to process significant loss?
1.

2.

3.

What do you believe is God's way of handling this area?
1.

2.

3.

9. Expressing Anger

How did your parents express anger?
1.

2.

3.

What did your parents do when someone was angry?
1.

2.

3.

What did your parents say or teach about anger?
1.

2.

3.

10. Parenting and Children

What did your parents do to train or control their children?
1.

2.

3.

What did your parents say about their role as parents or your role as children?
1.

2.

3.

What was communicated about having children?
        Joy, duty, drudgery, etc.
1.

2.

3.

11. God and Religion

What did your parents model about God and religion?
1.

2.

3.

What type of spiritual practices or religion did your parents practice?

1.

2.

3.

What did your parents teach or say about God and religion?

1.

2.

3.

What was confusing about their approach to God and religion?

1.

2.

3.

How involved were your parents in spiritual or religious practices?

1.

2.

3.

12. Conflict

How did your family deal with conflict?
1.

2.

3.

How was conflict resolved?
1.

2.

3.

What did your family do if someone remained in conflict?
1.

2.

3.

What do you believe is God's way of handling this area?
1.

2.

3.

13. Marriage and Singleness

What did your family say about being married or being single?

1.

2.

3.

How did your family treat married couples and single people?

1.

2.

3.

Was singleness an acceptable goal?

1.

2.

3.

Was marriage the ultimate goal?

1.

2.

3.

What do you believe is God's way of handling this area?
1.

2.

3.

14. Pleasure, Recreation, and Fun

What did your family do for fun?
1.

2.

3.

What did your family allow the individuals to do for fun?
1.

2.

3.

How much money and time was given to recreation or fun?
1.

2.

3.

What do you believe is God's way of handling this area?
1.

2.

3.

15. Race, Culture, Class

What did your family communicate about your race, culture, or class?
1.

2.

3.

What did your family communicate about others of a different race, culture, or class?
1.

2.

3.

16. Authorities and Power
What did your parents model in relation to authorities?
1.

2.

3.

What did your parents teach or say about authorities?

1.

2.

3.

How did your parents react to an authority stopping them from doing something?

1.

2.

3.

17. Politics

What was your parents' attitude toward politics?

1.

2.

3.

What did your parents say about politics?

1.

2.

3.

What were your parents' political views?

1.

2.

3.

One of the key things that these questions will reveal is that we have significant amount of programming from our family, culture, or significant figures in our lives. The way they did things becomes the way we do things whether their way was good, bad, or ineffective. The key question in this arena is: Are you learning, examining, and growing in wisdom to evaluate the best way to respond in the various circumstances of life. God has given us in the Scriptures His way of responding to life. It is His wisdom that will allow us to have a blessed life.

.

Secret #4

Hunger and Thirst for Righteousness

MATTHEW 5:6
*Blessed are those who
hunger and thirst after righteousness
for they shall be satisfied.*

4
Hunger and Thirst for Righteousness

Years ago I had the privilege of meeting Corrie Ten Boom who helped shelter Jews during the days of the Holocaust during WWII in Holland. She was absolutely radiant in her love of Jesus Christ, even in her old age. I have also had the privilege of studying under Dr. Francis Schaeffer in L'Abri, Switzerland, as he helped return deep philosophical thinking to the Christian Church as a whole. He was amazing in his ability to think and love deeply. These are two heroes of mine for the unique work that they did to fight injustice and move Christianity forward. When I think of heroes, I also think of William Wilberforce and John Wesley who helped end slavery and brought the gospel to the poor. I think of Clara Barton who started the Red Cross and Florence Nightingale who brought new levels of nursing care to wounded veterans of war. Each of these heroes became dedicated to a particular issue or righteous cause that needed to be done. This is what heroes do—they champion righteousness.

Have you met any real heroes? Let me introduce two modern-day heroes. Don Brewster and Jenny Williamson are heroes because they both have heard a call from God to help change the world in regard to sex trafficking. Don Brewster sold his house in America and moved to Cambodia to start rescuing girls who were being sold for sex. Don has made huge progress against this great evil. Jenny Williamson started rescuing young girls who were being bought and sold in California. Jenny has started a

120

movement to repair the broken lives of these girls and no longer ignore this huge problem. Both of these people are remarkably alive and sparkle with purpose as they work against a great moral evil. In both of their cases they were minding their own business when this cause found them. They heard the voice of God to engage with this cause. There are other causes and problems in the world, but they know that they are to engage on this one issue. Jesus tells us that we cannot be truly blessed until we are hungering and thirsting to see righteousness expressed. I believe that everyone has a purpose, a destiny, and a righteousness that they need to jump in on.

I bring up these two folks because they have this deep happiness that Jesus talks about because they are doing their righteousness. Yours may not be to jump in on this injustice. Your life may need to be focused on some other injustice or crucial issue in our world. The list is almost endless: prisoners, corrupt government, the homeless, addiction, fatherlessness, orphans, poverty, women's rights, church planting, leprosy, HIV, environmental issues, micro-finance, animal cruelty, financial literacy, literacy, education, etc. But Jesus is completely right that we will not experience a deeply happy life until we are pushing hard for something that is bigger than ourselves.

Who are the real heroes in our world? It isn't the plastic people who are into themselves and preen for the cameras. The real heroes are those people who have given themselves to something that really matters. They sacrifice, plead, act, motivate, and do whatever it takes to see their cause take significant steps forward. If you don't know your cause, then you aren't ready to live. Sometimes the issue can seem rather small to others - like living so that your children or village can have a better life.

God has some project, cause, issue, or injustice that He wants you to jump in on. We become alive in a different way when we begin to hunger and thirst for a particular righteousness that we have become alerted about. In Don and Jenny's case they both feel that God specifically directed them to jump in on the issue of sex trafficking. But for many people they will try engaging on this issue or that issue, and it won't seem to click. But that is okay. Keep trying to make a difference and keep trying out various causes and issues. One day one of them will just click. The people who are involved, the cause itself, your experience with it, your expertise in some aspect of the work, and you will find yourself embracing this hunger and thirst for a particular righteousness that will change your life.

I have watched many people enjoy the flow of this type of cause and issue and then back away from it because they are older or moving into a different stage of life. Now I am all for evaluating our lives for balance and effectiveness on the highest priorities but do not back away from a great issue so you can spend more time in front of the television or another silly, selfish pursuit. Too often these transitions are opportunities for selfishness or self-focus to take control. If you back away from righteousness to pursue some selfish or self-focused pursuit, you will miss this blessing and miss a new level of life.

Jesus tells us that one of the keys to a blessed and deeply happy life is to have a deep desire for righteousness. This desire has to burn within you to the place it is like hunger and thirst. Most of us do not see this as a key to becoming deeply happy, but God does. He knows that until you are involved in the righteous causes, moral behaviors, and personal purpose He created you for, then you will never be truly happy. He will engineer circumstances, allow you to be exposed to people, and force you to experience difficulty all with the purpose to bless you. If He knows that you will never be truly happy until you are dialed in on your righteous purpose, He has to keep nudging you toward those forms of righteousness. I have watched people avoid the causes, morality, and/or purposes which would make them truly happy. It is like they are walking past a pile of gold nuggets, but they don't want to stop and pick any up. They think that cause is beneath them. They think it will be too hard to make a difference. They think that it is impossible for them to start being moral. They believe that they are past the time they can make a U-turn and stop being evil. They pretend that they don't care about anyone but themselves. They think the problem is too big and they are too small, and their little efforts won't help. All the while they are missing out on some of the greatest joys in life.

Pursuing Righteousness

Jesus tells us that a blessed life awaits those who will pursue righteousness with a reckless abandon. There seems to be at least four forms of righteousness that He means. The first is ultimate righteousness which is the perfection that gets a person into heaven. The second, third, and fourth type of righteousness grow out of the Great Commandments that Jesus tells us are the marching order for all of life. The first of these is to love God with all your heart, soul, mind, and strength. The second of these great commandments is to love ourselves righteously so that we will have the energy and balance to love others. The third of these great commandments is to love others righteously.

The Ultimate Righteousness

The ultimate goal of all righteousness is to secure a place in heaven with God someday. God has told us that there are two ways to obtain ultimate righteousness and be fit for heaven.

Listen to Romans 3:21-26:
But now apart from the Law the righteousness of God has been manifested, being witnessed by the Law and the Prophets, even the righteousness of God through faith in Jesus Christ for all those who believe; for there is no distinction; for all have sinned and fall short of the glory of God, being justified as a gift by His grace through the redemption which is in Christ Jesus; whom God displayed publicly as a propitiation in His blood through faith. This was to demonstrate His righteousness, because in the forbearance of God He passed over the sins previously committed; for the demonstration, I say, of His righteousness at the present time, so that He would be just and the justifier of the one who has faith in Jesus.

There is the "earn your way" to heaven by being the absolutely perfect way of getting ultimate righteousness and a place in heaven. The problem with this pathway to righteousness is that no one has been able to fulfill the requirements except God Himself. No one is gaining ultimate righteousness on their own through their actions and decisions.

The second way of gaining ultimate righteousness is as a gift from God. He tells us that if we believe Him and follow Him, then He will give us the gift of the righteousness that we could never earn. Our faith in God activates the gift of ultimate righteousness. It is important to state that this is an active faith not just intellectual ascent. When we believe in Jesus Christ as Savior and Lord, we actively pursue Him.

If you have never put your trust in Jesus Christ as your only means for obtaining ultimate righteousness, heaven, and peace with God, then pray a prayer like the one below:

Dear Heavenly Father

I do hunger and thirst after your approval and the righteousness that only you can provide. I thank you for providing your Son, the Lord Jesus Christ, to live a perfect life and then die on the cross for me in my place. I accept His payment for my sins and trust in His work as my ticket into heaven. I want the Lord Jesus Christ to come into my life and make me the kind of person you want me to be. I am trusting in Jesus Christ and following Him as my way to be righteous and forgiven.

In the Name of the Lord Jesus Christ,
Amen

Actualized Righteousness

Jesus was essentially asked by a young seeker of truth, "What should I do with my life?" His answer was very instructive. He defines actualized righteousness. He tells us the framework for all of life. He says in Matthew 22:37-39 that all of life should be about three commands (we call these the great commandments) – Love God, Love Self, and Love Others. His answer gives us a picture of actualized righteousness. We know that we will not achieve the perfection of God. That must be received as a gift from God through our faith. But there is righteousness that we must pursue here on earth that helps us obtain the blessing that Jesus talks about in the Beatitudes. In order to actualize this righteousness that Jesus wants us to pursue in this life, one must follow Jesus' prescriptions in the great commandments.

How are you pursuing God so that it is clear that He is number one in your life? How are you loving God with all your heart, soul, mind, and strength? What does this actually look like in your life? Clearly, in order to participate in this command, we must find a way to constantly and regularly be in pursuit of God. For over 2,000 years serious Christians (Jewish believers for even longer) have pursued God through the practice of the spiritual disciplines. These disciplines allow you to attend to God in every part of your day and life. This has been a time-tested way to love God while allowing Him to work His work of sanctification in us. I have laid out some of these classic spiritual disciplines in the exercise below. I make the case for these spiritual disciplines in my book, *Spiritual Disciplines of a C.H.R.I.S.T.I.A.N.* I do not believe that it is possible to have deep love of Jesus that fulfills God's command to love God with all your heart, soul, mind, and strength without utilizing these spiritual practices regularly. Each person will respond to specific practices differently, but these spiritual exercises are a time tested way of practicing our faith. Some disciplines will bring the delight of God's presence to one person while it may leave another person cold spiritually. Try these various disciplines and see which ones allow you to enjoy deeper levels of your love for God. Each of the disciplines acts as notes in a symphony of your love for God. God wants you to draw near to Him and let His presence invade every part of your life.

Exercise #1

Please check the spiritual disciplines that you regularly practice:

o **Confession:** This is the practice of agreeing with God about our personal sins, our family sins, our national sins, and our cultural sins. It is based upon 1 John 1:9 but examples abound in Scripture.

o **Guidance of the Holy Spirit:** This is the practice of listening for the subjective prompting of the Holy Spirit. Galatians 5:16, Ephesians 4:30; Isaiah 30:21

o **Bible Study:** This is the practice of analyzing the Scriptures in detail and drawing out of it truths, insights, applications, and encouragement that God wants to bring into our lives.

127

○ **Biblical Meditation:** This is the process of ruminating on Scripture passages in various ways in order to press the Scriptural truths through your mind, will, emotions, spirit, and body. Psalm 1:1-3; Joshua 1:8; Colossians 3:15-16; Colossians 3:1-12.

○ **Prayer:** This is the many-faceted process of interacting with God. There are many ways of talking and interacting with God. It is very helpful to explore many of these pathways before you desperately need them. A person must have a number of ways of interacting with God back and forth so that a real relationship can form.

○ **Worship:** This is the practice of giving praise, adoration, thanksgiving, and reverence to God Almighty. This has both a private and a corporate aspect that should be practiced regularly.

○ **Fellowship:** This is the practice of engaging deeply with three other types of believers: those who know more than you, those who are about equal with you spiritually, and those who know less than you.

○ **Service:** This is the practice of being open to the direction of God in at least three arenas: spontaneously at God's prompting every day; using your spiritual gifts, natural abilities, or available time to help the church; and to let the larger community know that God loves them.

○ **Communion:** This is the practice of reminding ourselves of the key element in our relationship with God: the life, death, and resurrection of Christ.

o **Baptism**: This is the practice of identifying ourselves with the Triune God, the death of Christ, and an appeal to God for a clean conscience.

o **Witnessing**: This is the practice of telling others about what God has done for you.

o **Fasting**: This is the practice of not eating for some period of time in order to focus on prayer and spiritual issues.

o **Solitude**: This is the practice of not being with others for some period of time for prayer and/or spiritual issues.

o **Silence**: This is the practice of not speaking for some period of time for the practice of prayer or spiritual development.

o **Love**: This is the practice of letting God use your body, your words, your actions to meet the needs of others.

o **Generosity**: This is the practice of giving more than ten percent of your income to the Lord and others in need through tithes and offerings.

If you are unfamiliar with some of these disciplines, let me recommend my book, _Spiritual Disciplines of a C.H.R.I.S.T.I.A.N._, as a basic primer on these classic spiritual disciplines. This resource will help you learn how to pursue God in these various disciplines.

Ten Commandments

Another element of loving God is contained in what we should not do. We do not want to offend God or shame Him by the way we act or speak. We cannot earn our way into heaven or impress God by trying to keep within the Ten Commandments but staying within these boundaries are acts of love and righteousness. The Ten Commandments are a list of limits that mark the boundaries of loving behavior in His eyes. A righteous understanding of love means that love for God and others must be within the boundaries of the Ten Commandments. A man cannot say that he loves his wife and that is why he is having an affair. An employee cannot say that they love their company and that is why they are stealing from it. A person can't say that they love their neighbor and that is why they are lying about them in court. A parent can't say that they love their child and that is why they are abusing them with swear words. The moral boundaries around a righteous life are the Ten Commandments. It is absolutely essential to understand the basics of an ethical life.

Thou shalt not have any other gods before me
Thou shalt not make for yourselves any graven images
Thou shalt not take the name of the Lord thy God in vain
Remember the Sabbath day to keep in holy
Honor your Father and your Mother
Thou shalt not murder
Thou shalt not commit adultery
Thou shalt not steal
Thou shalt not bear false witness against thy neighbor
Thou shalt not covet anything that belongs to your neighbor

Are there any areas of your life where you are currently living outside of these moral boundaries?

What would it take to bring your life back inside of these guidelines? How long will it take you?

Who would you need to talk to in order to begin bringing your life back within the moral boundaries of God? Talk to whoever you need to talk with and begin the process of bringing your life back inside the place of safety and righteousness.

The Second Great Commandment

If we are serious about achieving the blessing that comes from hungering and thirsting after righteousness, then the next form of righteousness that we must pursue comes from the second great commandment. Jesus tells us that the second great commandment consists of two commands: loving ourselves righteously and loving our neighbor righteously. (Matthew 22:37-39). We often miss that he declares that we must take care of ourselves if we are to have the energy, resources, and knowledge to love our neighbors.

Righteously Loving Ourselves

If we are going to do justice to Jesus' second great commandment, then we are going to have to admit that it instructs us to love ourselves so that we can love others. If we have abused ourselves or continually neglect our own legitimate needs, then our love for others will come from a damaged place. It is important that we learn how to righteously love ourselves without indulging the selfish elements within us. This section will walk you through a number of exercises that help define and develop a righteous love of self.

Personal Growth Plan

If we are going to fully follow the righteous passions God has placed on our heart, then we will need to become all that we can be. We will need to have a growth and development plan that will not coddle us but will compel us forward to the kind of life we want and God wants for us. Each of us needs to have a growth and development plan if we are to maximize our leadership potential. If we do not keep growing, then we will begin to stagnate and regress. Below is a chart to help you determine your individualized plan for growth.

One of the easiest ways of looking at ourselves is to divide us up into four parts: our spiritual selves, our mental selves, our emotional selves, and our physical selves. We will look at exercises and projects in each of these areas so that we can become all we want to be and all God wants us to be.

1. Spiritual Growth Plan

For the purposes of this development plan let's talk about the spirit as the place of our creativity, the place of our conscience, the keeper of our sense of significance, the place of our connection to God. There may be other aspects of our spirit beyond these four, but let's begin with these four. The following projects and exercises will, through prayer, open you to more growth and development in these aspects of your spirit.

Creativity

I enjoy being creative with

1.

2.

3.

4.

5.

> I enjoy being creative with...
> and it recharges me when I...
>
> Woodworking, plants, film, fashion, writing, speaking, metal, water, organizations, finance, conversation, assisting others, trouble-shooting, computers, video games, modeling, animals, teaching, medicine, law, machinery, farming, electricity, management, leadership, ministry, etc.

We feed our spirit when we allow ourselves time to be creative. In our busy world more and more people find that they do not have time to do that thing that recharges them.

I plan on using and developing my originality and creativity in the following areas:

Conscience

I plan on developing and paying attention to my conscience in the following areas:

1.

2.

3.

4.

5.

Significance

I plan on increasing my personal sense of self-worth in the following ways:

1.

2.

3.

4.

5.

Intimacy with God

Check the spiritual disciplines that you plan on learning about and using this year to become more intimate with God.

- o Confessing

- o Yielding to the Holy Spirit

- o Reading, Memorizing, Studying, Meditating on Scripture

- o Praying

- o Fasting

- o Worshiping

- o Fellowship

- o Witnessing

- o Giving (Generosity)

2. Mental Growth Plan

The following are major areas of mental development with questions designed to help you think through how you are going to develop this next year and on into the future

1. How many books would you like to read this year? _____

2. Make a list of the topics you would like to explore through reading

   1.

   2.

   3.

   4.

   5.

   6.

   7.

   8.

   9.

   10.

3. How many audio programs do you plan to listen to weekly __, monthly___, yearly___?

4. What types of audio or video programs are you going to expose yourself to this year?

   1. Spiritual Growth
   2. Personal Development
   3. Marriage Improvement
   4. Parenting Improvement
   5. Vocational Improvement
   6. Ministry Development
   7. Community Development

5. How many seminars per year do you want to attend?
   _____

6. What types of seminars would you like to attend?

> 1. Spiritual Growth Seminars
> 2. Personal Development Seminars
> 3. Marriage Improvement Seminars
> 4. Parenting Improvement Seminars
> 5. Vocational Improvement Seminars
> 6. Ministry Development Seminars
> 7. Community Development Seminars

7. How many new people do you want to meet this year?

_____

Three general types of people
> 1. Those who can teach, instruct, or develop me.

_____

> 2. Those who are my peers, associates, colleagues.

_____

> 3. Those who I can serve, instruct, develop, help.

3. Emotional Growth Plan

The area of emotions is one in which we often do not realize that we can develop. But our emotional life is the key to our life. Our emotions are the reactions we have to the world as it is happening to us. We need to enjoy our emotions, control our emotions, harness our emotions, and release our emotions in righteous ways. The following is an expression of the major emotional areas so that you can think more deeply and realistically about your emotional development.

137

Depth

Our life becomes much richer when we begin experiencing the full range and depth of emotions that God created in us. In different ways and for different reasons we may have cut off our interaction with our emotions. This means that we may need to go back and develop our ability to experience our reactions to certain things in our world. Sometimes it can seem that we are weaker when we experience our emotions, but the opposite is true. When we can feel our emotions fully but not let them control us, we are much stronger and richer for the ability. Our lives were meant to have a rich, emotional tenor. This does not mean that we are angry or bitter or depressed, but that we are aware of that stream of reaction within us. Grow in your emotional depth. Grow in your ability to feel the reaction you are experiencing without being overwhelmed by it or completely lost in it.

Who will you see or what will you expose yourself to this year for the development of your emotional depth?

> Mission trip, Tijuana, children's hospital, skid row, police work, prisons, homeless shelter, animal shelter, etc.

Education

In what ways will you educate your emotional reactions? We all experience different things and at times our reaction is based upon incomplete information on why that is happening or it is culturally conditioned rather than informed. There may be emotions that regularly overwhelm you or significantly alter your possibilities.

138

Educate yourself about those emotions and the various places they could be coming from. Raw emotions are hard to handle and utilize for a

blessed life. Find a way to process the emotion so that it can become usable for you.

Who will you see or what will you do to educate yourself this year emotionally?

> Books, seminars, speeches, Scripture
> love, joy, peace, patience, kindness, goodness, etc.

Expression
We all need to work on our expression of emotions. We may have never learned how to control a particular emotion such as anger, and it just comes blurting out. We may have never let a particular emotion out for fear that we would be ridiculed or shamed. We may have never even realized our typical expression of an emotion is inappropriate for a new group we are trying to join or a new job we are trying to gain.

Who will you see or what will you do to change your emotions this year?

> Fear, anger, irritation, depression,
> worthlessness, passion,
> inferiority, romance, bitterness

Who will you see or what will you do to increase expression of your positive emotions?

4. Physical Growth Plan

Our bodies are the jar in which we hold the treasure of our spirit and soul as well as the wonder of Christ within us. We must take good care of our bodies or we will not be able to clearly follow the dictates of our soul and spirit and, more importantly, the Lord.

Exercise: What will you do this year to tone your body?
sit-ups, running, weights, basketball, walking, etc.

1.
2.
3.
4.
5.

Skill: What new skill do you hope to acquire this year?
golf, skiing, flying, tennis, carpentry, sewing, etc.

1.
2.
3.
4.
5.

Diet: What will you do this year that will make your diet healthier? Eliminate: sweets, sodas, seconds, red meat, etc. Add more: fiber, salads, vegetables, vitamins, etc.

1.
2.
3.
4.
5.

The Re-Energizing Cycle

One of the consistent issues in pursuing righteousness is keeping our energy up and not allowing ourselves to become exhausted. We become more susceptible to temptation and other unwise decisions when we allow ourselves to become physically and/or spiritually exhausted. A number of years ago in my role as District Superintendent supervising pastors I had the responsibility of working with pastors who had fallen morally. It is never an easy assignment to investigate moral failure and then work with a church to remove a pastor if it is true. In the midst of the investigations I conducted, I noticed a trend. Every pastor who fell into sin told me that they were exhausted and the affair, the embezzlement, the gambling, the sin was the only thing that gave them the energy to continue. The exhaustion was a constant. I do not believe that sin is the only way to energize an exhausted person, but I do believe it is a very convenient way.

What do you do when you are exhausted? The pace and demands of life constantly drain us, and we need to have a realistic and well thought-through plan to re-energize ourselves constantly. Most often we are not aware of how exhausted we are until we hit bottom or do something stupid that we would not normally do in an effort to have some energy back in our life. Rather than be drawn into sin, let's walk through the crucial arenas where we can be replenished in positive ways. We so often neglect our own needs that we do not treat ourselves righteously. I have found that the following eight arenas needed to be watched. Think of this as a hidden checklist that will keep you from being susceptible to foolish and sinful ideas. Before we become exhausted with little way to make it back, spend time with these practical areas and how they need to be arranged in your life.

A number of years ago I was introduced to an idea that was so helpful that I needed to include it in this section. They called it the Replenishment Cycle. I became aware of the idea through the Patterson Center and their excellent Life Planning process. They ask you what replenishes you and you figure it out with your life planning coordinator. I would highly recommend that you consider having a life plan developed from this excellent group. I have taken their idea and added to it a little more structure. I have found that certain elements need to be considered. These eight elements seem to be universal in their ability to re-energize. These are not quick charges but instead are slow trickle charges that help us stay energized in the midst of our life's demands. Car mechanics tell us that you can only jolt a battery back to life so many times without doing significant damage. What batteries need is a slow trickle charge that recharges them over some time. The same is true for us as humans. There may be many more things that help replenish you as you move through life, but these eight can be a start.

Matthew 11:28-30

Come unto Me all you who are weary and heavy laden and I will give you rest. Take my yoke upon you and learn of Me for I am gentle and humble of heart. For My yoke is easy and my burden is light.

I have put these eight concepts in a wheel diagram to help you see that these are the ways to recharge your life and get it spinning at its maximum level. You may require much more space than I have provided in this diagram to really look at this area and how you can be recharged in this area. Take a blank sheet of paper and write down all the ideas that come to mind as we cycle through these eight arenas.

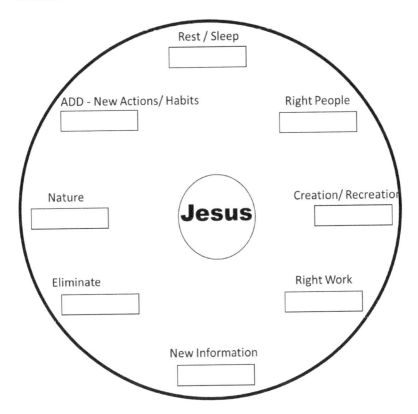

Filling in the Re- Energizing Cycle

Now that you can see the eight arenas that re-energize people, let's begin looking at these areas in more detail. You will need to think through what things in this area push energy back into you.

1. Rest and Sleep

How much rest and sleep do you really need? This is an obvious need, but so often we constantly get less sleep than we actually require to be at our peak. Don't write down how much you can afford to get. Write down what you really need every night to feel rested. You will have to decide how to get that much later.

Let me give you a personal example. I have found that I need seven full hours of sleep each night and a nap of about a half an hour each day. Without this level of sleep, I begin to wear down. I can get less for a short period of time; but if when I do this for too long, the people around me suffer and I begin to notice I am not as creative or energetic.

2. Right People

Who are the right people that energize you and encourage you? We all have people who energize us and those who drain us. We need to increase the amount of time we spend with energizers and decrease the amount of time with those who drain us. This can be a dangerous list, but you must make it mentally and sometimes actually write it down. Who are the people when you are done spending time with them, you are recharged and full of energy? And who are those people who when you spend time with them, you are drained?

Sometimes the people who drain us are those who are closest too us who have developed a negative orientation. We need to change the nature of that relationship or move away from that person as much as possible. I can remember in one work environment there was one guy who could just drain people with his demands, point of view, and disrespect. I had to interact with this person, but I found a way to minimize it to one hour per week.

3. Creation and Re-Creation

What do you like to do creatively? What fun activities bring life and joy back to you? All of us need to do things weekly that bring delight and energy to us. It is different for everybody as to what it might be, but we all need it. It could be a hobby or some creative pursuit. It could be sports or bird watching. In most people's life it is a list of things that they need to do over the course of a year. There is not usually just one thing that will completely recharge you.

One of the places to look is at those areas where you are creative. God has said we are made in His image and He is creative. We express some element of His image in us when we are creative. This could be photography, woodworking, writing, dance, building, drawing, designing, or a thousand other things. But all of us are creative in some ways and these need to be a part of our normal cycle of life.

4. Right Work

What kind of work brings you joy and energy? Are you spending more than 30 – 50 percent of the time doing things at your work that drain you? Most of us have the ability to adjust our jobs to some degree or get a different job if the one we have is draining the life from us. No amount of money is worth being a zombie when the work day is done.

What would you do with your life if money was not a need? What kind of difference would you like to make?

Many of us don't have the chance to be paid right away for what we are the most passionate about, but we can come up with a plan to get us working in that field in a few steps. Take control of your life and start working in an area that energizes you. Then find out the kind of actual work that gets you revved up.

If you are in a job that drains you and there are little to no options to ever get out of the specific work that drains you, then you may have to have the courage to quit. Find a different job that energizes you. Move in the direction of work that is stimulating and invigorating to you.

5. New Information

What new sources of information are helping you, educating you, and directing you so you avoid the mistakes of the past? It is important to always be growing and learning. We often fall into patterns that work for us in certain situations, but they will not work if our life gets busier or more complex. We need to look at new systems. We need to learn new information that will inform the way we think about life. In most cases our life is stuck in the places it is stuck because of how we are thinking about that area or relationship. If we could think differently, it would open up all kinds of new possibilities.

It is this new information and new skills that you must begin to acquire that will re-energize you. In most cases we don't know what we don't know so the only way to find the areas where we need new information is in the areas that are not going well. If your work life is not what it could be, then dedicate some new time to gaining information about work. If your marriage or family is not an enjoyable place, then dive into those arenas and begin learning how to handle it different. If you are constantly short of money, then dedicate yourself to learning the rules of money. It is amazing what new information will do to your stress level.

6. Eliminate

What people, activities, or jobs do you need to eliminate from your life because they drain you or are toxic in some way to you? This is always an interesting question because people often don't think they can change anything about their life. But if there is a person who constantly drains you, then figure out how to change that about your interaction or minimize your time with that person or eliminate them from your life. Many people hate their jobs but do not look for a new one. In most cases you should not quit your current one until you have your next one but changing jobs and even career fields is the best move you can make for your health and energy.

One of the things that many people find is that it is the little activities, the little jobs, the little interactions that need to be eliminated. Sometimes you need to eliminate checking the news right before your bedtime. Sometimes you need to stop checking emails or messages. Sometimes you need to remove an hour or two of TV. Sometimes you need to resign from the nonprofit board you sit on. Sometimes you need to hire out your gardening or house or car repair. Sometimes you need to stop hanging out at the bar with the folks from work. Sometimes you need to eliminate dessert or bread. Sometimes you need to eliminate the heavy lunch or the big treat after dinner.

7. Nature

What types of exposure to nature energize you? God seems to have wired us to be recharged by nature. It could be being on a lake or feeling the waves crash against your legs at the beach. It could be hiking in the forests or walking through a rose garden. Something about the beauty, the cleanliness, the splendor of God's raw creation begins to put back into us what is being taken out by our life.

Different people respond to nature differently. What works for one person may be a draining experience for another. Usually when I ask about nature, people can fairly quickly tell me the kind of exposure to nature that recharges them. Write down what does it for you. It is okay if it is different from your partner or your friends.

Be ready to explore new ways to be in or around nature that you have not tried. As we grow older, we may not be able to hike twenty miles anymore, but we can do other things that replenish us. Start by writing down anything you would like to do in nature but haven't done. Continue with the things that intrigue you as possibilities.

8. Add

What do you need to add to your life to make you or your life more energized and joyful? This seems simple enough, but it is so often overlooked. There are activities, people, events, and things that we can add to our life; and they would be incredibly recharging. Have you always wanted to go to a particular concert? Is there a trip you have wanted to take? What are the things that would just bring delight to your life if you purchased them?

Recently my wife and I had the privilege of taking a dream trip that we have been hoping to take for 10+ years. We went sailing through the Greek Isles to many of the places where the Apostle Paul went on his missionary journeys. We ran across a brochure for a trip to do that, and we prayed that God would give us the money. The money came in through a tax refund almost to the penny and we decided to go. It was delightful and incredibly beneficial for our souls. We are still aglow from that trip over nine months later.

Recently I was facing a need to purchase another commuter vehicle and rather than doing something normal, I decided to save money and have some fun at the same time. I bought a motor scooter for my commute. It has proven to be an incredible delight. I can't stop smiling when I am dashing around on it, and it gets 100 miles to the gallon. I believe that we need to look for these ways to bring a little zest and energy back to the day to day.

We so often only look at sinful things as ways to have fun: drinking, sensuality, gambling, etc. These are not really energizing; they are jolts of electricity that ultimately leave your drained. There are lots of righteous things that we can do to add a whole new level of energy and joy to our lives. Keep on the lookout for these little righteous things to add to your life.

9. Jesus

What ways can you bring Jesus into your life in new ways to unload some of the burdens and exhaustion? Jesus tells us in Matthew 11:28-30 to bring our weariness to Him. He says that He can help us untie the loads that we have added to our life. He wants to train us to live a different way – a way that does not have the constant strain and bring a mind-numbing weariness.

First, we need to make sure that we have asked Jesus to carry our sins and guilt. Too many people are still trying to pay for their own sins and assuage their own guilt. The Bible tells us that that is what Jesus came to do. He is the Lamb of God who takes away the sins of the world. We need to stop trusting in our works our religiosity and put all our trust in what Jesus did for us on the cross. We have no hope of heaven if we are counting on ourselves, but we have the confident assurance that if we trust in Jesus Christ as our Savior, then we will be accepted into the family of God.

Second, we need to come to Jesus to learn a new way to live life rather than the selfish, competitive, self-sufficient way we have been living. Once we become a Christian, God wants us to let Jesus train us how to live in a humble and meek way. That is what this book is all about. God is trying to have us work out our salvation. Many times we have become Christians, but we are still striving for all the things of the world and not realizing that Jesus has a completely different way to live without the stress, pressure, and guilt.

Developing a Life Purpose Statement

Who does God want you to become? What is your maximum potential? All of these come together in your life purpose. In this section I want to suggest that you think through your gifts, talents, abilities, experiences, and education and combine them in to a statement which defines your life purpose. This defines what good works God has made for you to do while you are alive here on earth.

The following is my life-purpose statement that I have carried around for the last thirty years which has helped me define what I will and won't do:

"My purpose in life is to exhort, lead, and teach myself, my family, the church, and the world to live out God's principles of life by explaining truth in a compelling fashion; by showing how to embrace truth practically; and by leading people to a deeper commitment to and discovery of Jesus Christ."

Your purpose statement will be different, but it will become a guiding light of what to do and what to avoid. This is the genius of your purpose statement. It helps you know what you should pursue and what you shouldn't pursue. Start eliminating all the things that do not help you accomplish that God-ordained purpose.

Write out your own life purpose:

Include your dominant gifts, talents, abilities, experiences, education, and direction.

Righteously Loving Others

Jesus says in this Beatitude that every one of us has at least one righteous cause, issue, organization, institution that we are supposed to champion and help to move forward during our lifetimes. Our life is not supposed to be only about ourselves. We must, in a number of ways, give ourselves to a cause that is bigger than ourselves. We make ourselves most ready for heaven when we live beyond the boundary of our selfishness.

Our righteous cause will always be bigger than any one individual. Usually God has placed a dream in our heart that will aid that cause in some way. If we are going to have a blessed life, we need to find that righteous cause that we were made to assist. For some it may be the family, for some it could be children, for some it could be education, for some it could be justice for a particular group, for some it could be the church, for others it could be political, for some it could be about animals, for some it could be governmental, for some it could be a mission. But each of us has at least one of these causes that we need to get behind and help.

There are all kinds of incompletes and evil in the world that you are supposed to be involved in solving. God has designed you to make a difference in those areas. Your future depends upon your embracing these causes, issues, and purposes. You can make a difference.

We are not responsible to love everyone in the world. We are responsible to love the people in our world.

I have included a number of exercises that will help you develop a righteous love for others.

The 5-10 exercise

To love others means to meet their needs, to pursue their soul, and to please them in appropriate ways. What am I doing to meet the needs of, pursue, and please those closest to me? I have found that we are often far too vague about what we need to do to love the people in our lives. It is more helpful to actually list the ways that we are loving these people and then show the list to the people themselves and see if that is what they would define as love. What five to ten specific things am I doing regularly to really love the people in my life?

I have found that when you boil it down, there are only a few things that you need to do to keep a relationship really healthy; but you do have to do them. For illustration purposes let me share with you what my actual list is for two of my relationships. This is the list of what I actually think about making sure I do in these relationships.

The first relationship I want to share my 5-10 key actions is my relationship with my spouse, Dana, who is a wonderful woman, wife, mother, and friend. Here are my ten things that I have on the forefront of my mind to do for her every day or every week.

1. Compliment - every day

2. Say I love you – every day

3. Pass her test – to see if she is more important than something else

4. Listen for an hour – every day

153

5. Apologize

6. Earn money and manage the money

7. Never argue – there are always options

8. Plan dates and family outings

9. Align expectations constantly

10. Defend her from threats

I have written a whole book on how to construct this list for loving your wife based upon the Scriptures. If you want to explore the biblical ideas behind this plan and further details and exercises you can pick up my book, *God's Radical Plan for Husbands*. My wife and I also wrote a book for wives called *God's Radical Plan for Wives*.

The second relationship I want to talk about is my relationship with God. I have only eight actions on my list that keeps my relationship with Him fresh, inviting, and new. Other things might happen during the day or week as God and I relate, but these are the things I make sure that happen. These may not be the ways God will lead you, but I want you to see that it is not rocket science to keep a relationship healthy; you just have to be doing a few right things. Now let me be clear theologically. It is not what I do that begins or maintains my relationship with God. IT IS ALL HIM. But if I do not do my little part, then I do not receive the benefit of all that He has done.

1. Spend one hour every day with Him

2. Thank God for my blessings

3. Ask Him how to handle my problems

4. Listen to His answers in Proverbs, Psalms, stories of the Bible and other parts of the Bible

5. Practice other spiritual disciplines

6. Learn more about Him, myself, and others from the Bible

7. Worship with other people weekly

8. Use my spiritual gift as often as possible

If you want to understand this area of deeper relationship with God, then let me refer you to my book *Spiritual Disciplines of a C.H.R.I.S.T.I.A.N.* I detail in this book how to practice the various spiritual disciplines and how to build your own unique walk with God.

Spouse:
1.
2.
3.
4.
5.

Family:
      Children
      1.
      2.
      3.
      4.
      5.

      Parents
      1.
      2.
      3.
      4.
      5.

      Relatives
      1.
      2.
      3.
      4.
      5.

Work:

Colleagues

1.
2.
3.
4.
5.

Bosses

1.
2.
3.
4.
5.

Subordinates

1.
2.
3.
4.
5.

Friends:

1.
2.
3.
4.
5.

Four Basic Areas of Righteousness

All of us have been wired to respond to at least one of four basic categories of righteous compassion: Recovery, Prevention, Justice, or Development. It is evident all around us that the world is a broken place. Each of us is to wade into this life and make a positive difference before our life is over. This is a part of our purpose for being here. Jesus says that without this embrace of the righteousness which we are to create, we will not be satisfied. There is something deeply satisfying when we do what is righteous. Our family would go the Downtown Rescue Mission to serve food to the homeless on Saturday nights. One evening we took a neighbor girl with us for the first time. She waded in and helped hand out a healthy meal to those who lived on the streets. When the evening was finished, she turned to me and said, "My heart feels really good doing this." This is what righteousness does. It blesses those who do it.

The first area of righteousness that needs to be considered as a part of your purpose in life is helping recover those who have been broken by life. Many people find their calling in life by working with those who have hurts, hang-ups, or habits that are destroying their lives. Life can be brutal and all of us need help from time to time and some need lots of help getting back on their feet after major issues. There are an almost endless number of ways of making a difference in the lives of those who need recovery. Jump in and see where you could help. If you were to help a group of people who needed recovery work, which group would you want to work with?

The second area of righteousness that needs to be considered as a part of your purpose in life is preventing people from making damaging decisions. We live in a world full of dangerous choices. Some of the choices that we can make will destroy whole sections of our potential. I have noticed that a number of people have a calling to help people not make these kind of bad decisions. Their advice, guidance, and help can be in any number of arenas: spiritual, verbal, vocational, leadership, anger, racial, sexual, property, honesty, planning. People who move into this arena hope to help people before they make disastrous decisions and need the people in the first group. Some of these people specialize in passing laws; others build companies and/or technology that prevents people from making some decisions.

If you could prevent people from making bad decisions, which bad decisions are you most interested in preventing?

The third area of righteousness that needs to be considered as a part of your purpose in life is seeking justice against those who perpetrate harm and damage on others. There are evil people in the world who seek their advantage without any thought to the destruction that it causes or may cause to others. These people who initiate damage to others to gain for themselves must be stopped. Some people feel a special call to stop these damaging people. God raises up lots of these types of righteous people to expose the evil, to stop the evil, and to punish the evil. If God has called you to this form of righteousness, then your blood boils when people do evil to others and you want to be a part of stopping people like that. There are all kinds of ways of being involved in justice from journalism to police to courtrooms.

If you could bring a certain kind of person to justice or expose a certain evil, who would these people be and/or what is the evil?

The fourth area of righteousness that needs to be considered as a part of your purpose in life is developing those who need to grow in order to seize their purpose in life. This kind of person sees people as bundles of potential. If they could just be developed, they could have a totally different life and make a huge righteous difference in the world. God plants deep in these people an unshakeable belief in the future potential of people. If you want to learn and if you will put in the effort, then the sky is the limit for everyone. Some of these people work with the children; some with the teens; some with the adults – but it is always about developing that person to their maximal potential for the greater cause of righteousness. Again the different ways that people can engage in this arena of righteousness is almost endless – from mentoring, to teaching, to employment, to listening, etc.

If you could work with any individual or group of people for their development ,who would the group be and what would you want to develop?

Righteous Causes

None of us will ever be satisfied with life until we are engaged in the cause(s) for which we were created. That cause has to go beyond ourselves and our families. It is about righteousness and the kingdom of God. It may involve children or prisoners. It may be about teenagers or senior citizens. It may be about relief for disasters or about human slavery; but whatever it is, it is in every one of us and we need to be about making a change in that arena. It may be about prevention or recovery or justice, but it is about righteousness. If we ignore our desires to help our fellow man and the stewardship of the world we have been given, then we will shrink as a being and miss God's best in our life.

Yes, everyone is busy and it is not easy to make a difference; but if everyone gets involved, then much good can be accomplished. God has left our world unfinished and capable of great good and great evil. It is our job to be a part of finishing our societies and cultures in a righteous way instead of allowing selfishness to win.

If you could be a part of stopping one kind of evil, preventing one type of mistake or sin, recovering a certain type of person or developing one type of person or a skill within a willing learner, what would it be?

How much time do you spend in making that happen?

A general rule of thumb is to spend two hours a week serving God in the church and two hours a month out in the community.

Secret #5

Mercy

MATTHEW 5:7
Blessed are the merciful for they shall receive mercy

5
Mercy
Developing a Forgiving Heart

I learned some of my first lessons about the power of mercy on the track team even though that is not what I thought I was learning. I went out for the track team after the coach recruited me. I thought when I showed up for my first practice that I would be welcomed as a hero. I wasn't. I was put in a group of guys who were running quarter miles as hard as we could until we threw up. I was in the back of the pack, just trying to survive. We were running really hard, not getting enough rest, and then running another quarter mile. The fellow next to me, Tom, was the first to throw up. The coach applauded his effort. I had stepped into a weird world where punishment was appreciated and you thanked your tormentors.

I don't ever remember hating my coach for all the torturous things he had us do. I have been on many teams since then and every coach has put us through drills, training, and pain. And we thanked him. Never once do I remember any of us getting mad at the coach for making us work hard or practice something over and over. We wanted to win. Winning meant being in shape and having the ability to push through difficulty to make the key play.

This sounds ridiculous if it is taken outside of the world of sports or the military, but in a sense this is what Jesus is telling us is one of the secrets to a deeply happy life. Jesus tells us that you will not really be happy until you have this active quality called mercy. Biblical mercy is such a rich word that it takes five or six words to fully describe it: kindness, lovingkindness, goodness, grace, favor, compassion, pity, steadfast love. But in each case it is a positive, active, outgoing word. Mercy is not passive; it does not let things happen – it loves, does good, and is kind. It swallows the wrong of others in love, kindness, and goodness. There will be people who hurt you, abuse you, and actively do evil to you. But mercy seeks to see them in a completely different light. Mercy is an active quality that lets go of the pain, evil, and injustice and embraces the positives that can come from the training. The word bitterness comes from the Hebrew root marar which means to be bitter, difficult, hard, miserable; but it also can mean to strengthen, to toughen, and/or to make strong. In Exodus 1:14, the slavery of Egypt was said to have made their lives stronger and tougher. You have to see your tormentors or punishers as part of a larger plan and trying to do something good for you.

Now this is not to say that those who perpetrate evil against another human being should not be stopped or punished. Of course they should be stopped; but in order to not let the evil that the individual did enter your heart, we must mentally and spiritually embrace the truth that this was a workout to achieve some level of success in life. If I do not begin to actively see them in this merciful way, then my life will begin to center around their evil; it will infect me and change me in significant ways. I just listened to a pastor who was beaten for his faith and he told us that those seven men who beat him were gifts to strengthen his faith. He would not love Jesus as much if he had not been beaten. Yes, this is a mental trick. But it releases you from the cancer of bitterness that can destroy your life.

Mercy is an active quality that overwhelms evil with love, grace, favor, and kindness. It is not possible to enjoy deep happiness in this sinful world without the active quality of mercy. Our love must be stronger than our hurt. Our loving-kindness must be stronger than our focus on the pain they caused. When we hold on to the need to personally punish our tormentors, we rob ourselves of the real focus of winning at life.

There is a place for justice. But God says let Him have vengeance. Let Him deal with those who go beyond any lesson that God may have been trying to teach. Hand those people over to God and His appointed authorities. Take the workout and be successful. Yes, what they did may have been evil, illegal, unethical. Yes, it may need to be stopped from every happening again. But it is essential to see what could come from it and avoid building your life around the evil of others.

I failed at one of my later lessons in mercy when I was working for a soft drink company and my boss was assigned to my truck and hounded, screamed, and cursed at me all day for ten hours a day for over a week. I can remember hating him and wanting to give him a piece of my mind. He was treating me unfairly. I remember asking God if I could forget that I was a Christian for just a few minutes. I later learned to my shock that I was one of the quickest and most efficient truck drivers in that yard because of my bosses "training." I can remember when God prompted me to go back to him and thank him for how firm he had been in my training.

166

God has taken me, and I suspect you, through many coaching and training sessions to strengthen you for the success and joy He has planned in your life. If you are not careful, you will destroy all the value of the training by hating the person who applied the difficulty. It took me years to change my perspective on a man who told me to my face that he was dedicated to destroying my career. But in his attempts, God forced me to develop other skills, abilities and relationships that are why my life is so good today. I knew I was making progress when I could thank that man for all that God had done in my life through him.

The goal of forgiveness is to be free from the damaging impact of the past. We may always carry the scars of the wounds of the past, but we do not have to be imprisoned by these events and people. Many people underestimate the need for forgiveness. Without forgiveness we are not pursuing our mission in life; we are trying to pay back the injustice of others. Many allow bitterness to become their reason for living rather than letting go of the offenses of others and finding their true purpose and their unique positive contribution. The joy of forgiveness is the ability to move on with our lives and not let the evil of others keep haunting us. God never designed us to carry bitterness. There is healing in forgiveness. There is justice in forgiveness. As long as we keep trying to hold a person responsible for the wrong they did to us, God and His proper authorities will not be free to work. Forgiveness is a conscious choice. Forgiveness begins with the desire to be free of the weight of justice personally. The exercises and projects that are listed in this section are designed to have you process what has taken place in your life from various different angles and perspectives. Forgiveness involves three basic areas:

1) developing a forgiving heart that is able to let the offense go;

2) making sure that your conscience is clear in regard to this offense;

3) embracing the lessons and training that can come from this offense.

It is very easy to allow the evil that others do to us to become an open wound in our soul or a cancer that consumes all the good in our life. You can count on these people emerging in your life. In each phase of my life there has been someone there to try and wreck what I was hoping for. Let me give you just a glimpse into my life: In my teen years there was a popular boy at the school I went to who for six years would not let any of my classmates hang out with me or be my friend. He made sure that I was alone. In my twenties a few people made sure that I did not succeed with desired relationships and ministry opportunities. In my thirties, I had a man decide that I was not a good pastor and, therefore, dedicated himself to making sure that I never was offered another church to pastor. He did all he could to wreck my career as a pastor. God allowed these and many other injustices into my life. At each point I needed to get past what they did to me and move on to what God might be wanting me to learn. I needed to forgive them so that my feelings about them no longer controlled the choices I made.

I have watched people who have allowed their whole life to be twisted because of the evil of others. To not forgive is to give the other person control over your life. I have also watched people who have survived horrible evil and who have chosen to forgive. It is not easy and it does take time, but they become free and God blesses them with freedom in their soul. They can and do build a great life out of the ashes of what an evil person did to them. What they did was evil and should be punished, but the person must learn to forgive for their own sake. They need to be free from hating the people who did the evil.

While the exercises below may seem impossible or odd, they cause you to apply the principles of forgiveness found in the New Testament. This process will take time and will move you to think in new ways. However, being free from the enslaving attitudes of bitterness is worth it. Think of this time as being in a cocoon while you become a completely transformed person able to forgive people and not letting their selfishness derail your future.

Write out a list of those who have deeply wounded you.

It is often important to begin to focus on the specific people who have hurt you and the offenses that those people have done. Many people find that when they start to actually look at what the person, did it allows them to quantify this amorphous hurt more clearly. Most people do not have more than twenty people who have deeply wronged them; but if you do, then keep writing and noting what they did. Usually the list is rather small (less than ten people) who have deeply hurt you. We may have hundreds of people who have been rude, offensive, irritating, and/or bothersome; but we usually have few who really have wounded us or wronged us deeply. They may have hurt us in a number of different ways at a number of different times. I have left two pages for these individuals and their offenses. Over the next few exercises we will begin to process these offenses and these people to give you new ability to see them in new perspectives that will allow their impact in your life to lessen.

I would suggest that you write using initials or in some code that only you will know so that these painful memories stay private until you are ready to reveal them.

Person	Offense
1.	
2.	
3.	
4.	
5.	

What lesson, truth, insight, protection could come from this person or situation?

If we were to see these people as coaches or workout instructors, what lessons did you learn because of them? What things do you no longer do because of what they did? How could that be a positive? What things do you now do because of that experience or person? How did what they did push you into something else or challenge you? What lessons can you still learn from what they did? What truths, causes, insights are you sensitized to because of what they did?

In many cases it is overcoming what happened that has led to who you are and what you have accomplished. Every successful and well-adjusted person has had to overcome these kinds of events and people in their life. When I point out that these people who were offensive and even evil were responsible for some of the significant blessings in their life, people never want to admit that. I realize that the blessings came in spite of them but in some ways because of them. I know that there were some people who did everything they could to wreck part of my life, and it was because of what they did that God grew me in significant ways. We have this idea that we should only have easy coaches or nice coaches, but that is not always how some of our most significant growth takes place.

I also realize that in saying this I am pointing out that some of you are just beginning to overcome what was done to you. Any positive that could come from what happened to you is just beginning. I do not want to minimize the pain or evil you endured, but I do want to help you gain a different perspective. The positive side of the workout is just beginning as you process, grow, learn, overcome, and change. Keep growing and one day you may even be able to see good things growing out of this evil that you could never have imagined. Many have said after this kind of a process, "I would never have wished this on my worst enemy, but I am grateful for all that it did in my life."

Person Offense   Lessons, truth, insights, or growth

1.

2.

3.

4.

5.

Determine whether what they did was wrong or just offensive.

In the process of letting go of bitterness, it is important to label the nature of the offense. All societies have different levels of improper activities. These range from the criminal to the social. Let's spend some time looking at the types of offenses so we can label them more accurately.

These are general categories and the definitions are decidedly broad.

A criminal offense is where a person is harming others in some way and will most likely continue to harm others if they are not stopped. This would be like murder, rape, stealing, armed robbery, extortion.

A **civil offense** is where the person has harmed another person in some way, but they may not continue doing it to others. This might be where one neighbor damaged their neighbor's fence, car, or dog for some reason.

An **organizational offense** is where a person has offended, harmed, or hurt another person; but their actions were a part of an organizational policy, order, or decision. This might be where a person is fired or reprimanded or reassigned by their employer.

Unethical offenses are those offenses that are not technically or legally wrong, but they are clearly selfish and wound or put the offended in a bad position. This might be where a person lies about their age on a form to get a leg-up for a promotion or where a person uses their friendship with another person to push them ahead of a more qualified applicant for a promotion. An accidental offense is one in which the offender did not mean to do the action or did not understand that the action would result in what took place. This might be where a person did not know the brakes on the car were bad or they did not intend to lose control of the car as they sped out of the parking lot or they did not understand the power of the rifle or that it was loaded.

A **familial offense** is a wound, hurt, offense that takes place in a family or in a family's culture. This might be where a pet name used in a family becomes offensive to someone as they grow up. It may also be that a family ritual becomes offensive.

A religious offense is an offense where the particular rituals, restrictions, or understandings of a religion are violated or made to be violated. This may be where a person is made to listen to blasphemies about their faith practices. It may be where a person is made to participate or watch what is forbidden by their religion.

A personal offense is an offense that is personally offensive or harmful but not organizationally, civilly, or criminally liable. This may be a name or action that is used. It could be almost any action that another person continues to do after you have asked them to stop.

An everyday offense is an offense, hurt, or wound that regularly takes place but does not rise to ethical or legal standards of wrong. This might be a slight, a word, an action, or an attitude that demeans you or marginalizes you from your point of view. Sometimes we are wounded or offended by another's actions, but their actions were not wrong. They just irritated you or were offensive in some other personal way. However, if their offenses were criminally wrong or morally wrong, then you are to declare them as wrong.

Many people can never forgive or forget because they cannot label an offense as wrong. It might be because it is a loved one who committed it or because they feel responsible for the person. We must be willing to label an offense correctly. That was morally wrong!!! That was offensive!!! That was just irritating!!! That was criminal!!! Take each offense from the previous list and put it in a category below. Use the categories listed below to place the offense on a rough scale of evil. Let's take a look at the offenses in your life in more detail.

Who offended, wounded, or hurt you?	Which kind of offense was it?	What action needs to be taken to stop, process, or fix this offense?
Put the person's initials or name or some identifying mark	criminal, civil, organizational, unethical, accidental, familial, religious, personal, every day	If you don't know, put DK

Understand their basic selfish motive. (Luke 19:21)

All sin comes from a core point of selfishness within a person. So those who have sinned against you were in some way just acting selfishly. Most people who sin are not trying to damage others; they are just trying to get what they want without regard for the consequences it will cause. **We must come to see how selfishness was driving this other person to do what they did.** How was what they did selfish? It is important to realize that people have, at the core of their being, this principle of selfishness. Look at the list of the people and their offenses and identify the selfish thing the person was trying to do and say over them,

"Father, forgive them **for they know not what they do.**"

175

It was supposed to be merely a self-interest and self-preservation instinct that was sublimated to God's glory and others' good. But the fall of mankind stripped away our spiritual connection to God and made us lone wolves insensitive to others with our self-interest and self-preservation instincts dominant. It is only by inviting God back into your life and using His energy to direct and repair your relationships that we can achieve health in this world. Remember, other people will wound you because of some personal desire and not because they want to destroy you. Make sure you are clear about the motivation of the offense: forgetfulness, selfishness, accidental, pent-up anger, addiction, etc. There is usually one prime selfish motivation for an offense.

One of my favorite scenes in the *Count of Monte Christo* is when Edmund Dantes realizes that he was imprisoned for a crime he did not commit because of the selfishness of the chief prosecutor. There is an elation which comes from this knowledge. He is not a bad person who somehow deserved this imprisonment. No, the prosecutor was just protecting himself and being selfish. Then begins the way out of the prison he had been living in. God gives him the way out.

It is very common to hear people who have caused awful things to happen to say with all sincerity, "That is not what I intended to happen." Or, "That is not what I wanted to happen." The person was just focused on what they wanted and did not stop to think of all the downstream consequences of this one action.

Jesus acknowledges this orientation towards the sins of others when He says while hanging on the cross.

176

"Father, forgive them for they know not what they do." The people who were at that time crucifying him were just doing their jobs. They were being selfish even though they were killing the Son of God. He saw through their motives and asked the Father to pardon them because they did not understand the consequences of what they were doing.

I have asked many people to look at the offenses that have been done to them and to find the selfishness that always resides at the core of the offender's behavior. Why did this person do this thing? In most cases the person was not trying to damage others; they were just looking for what they wanted. It is true that at times a person does intentionally try to harm us, but even that grows out of a selfish motive.

Maturing from the Offenses of others

Romans 8:28, 29 says that God causes all things to work together for good for those who love God, to those who are called according to His purpose. It is very helpful to start listing the good things that have come from the offense, the good things that could come from the offense, or the good things that might have come from this offense.

I have given this assignment to many people over the years and it is always difficult to get started. We don't want to see any good in what was done to us. We want it to be all bad and justify our hate or bitterness. But God is powerful enough to bring good out of anything for those who love Him. He wants to begin to bring good out of your pain. It is not that the pain was necessarily good, but He can bring good out of it.

Look for the ways that God is trying to bless you. This is not saying that the offense was good; it was not. But God is powerful enough to bring good to you in spite of this horrible thing and sometimes out of this horrible thing. Start looking for the good and you will see it. Tell God that you want to know other ways this has been an open door for a blessing. For each offense list at least ten positive benefits.

As we have seen in the earlier exercises, some of our most important growth comes out of pain. With this exercise we begin a look at the ways that God may turn what is even an actual evil into a good. He chose to allow this person's choices to become real. They bear the responsibility for them but you carry the scars. But God can bring good even out of this.

Offense
1.
2.
3.
4.
5.
6.
7.
8.
9.
10.

Repeat this exercise for the other offenses that have been done to you. It is often in the looking for the good that we finally begin to see what has been there all along. You may need to return to this exercise over and over again in the years ahead as God gives you new perspectives and new insights. The manure pile of offenses that were done to you will yet grow flowers that will dazzle all those around you. Let God work and let the hate go. Let God fill you with hope for the future instead of hatred of the past.

Give vengeance to God completely: Romans 12:17; 13:4

A. Tell God your desires for your offender

Jesus tells us that we need to process the pain, loss, wounds, offenses, and sins of this life in Matthew 5:5 when He says "Blessed are those who mourn for they shall be comforted." Part of this processing of the pain may be telling God how devastated we were by the offense or how damaging the downstream consequences were of the offense. Another part of the mourning process is to tell God our feelings about the kind of punishments and justice we think should be done to the perpetrator. This is a therapeutic session between you and God where you are honest about the pain, the wound, and the changed life this person has caused. You bare your soul to God about the vengeance you think the person deserves. You are not scheming but suggesting. You know that ultimately God is the only one who can bring proper justice, but it is important that you bring your rage, bitterness, and thoughts out of yourself to the one being in the universe who can handle them. This was done by David in Psalms in what are called the Imprecatory Psalms. He rails against his

179

enemies and against the enemies of God. God can handle your raw emotions.

1.

2.

3.

4.

5.

6.

7.

8.

9.

10.

B. Tell God you will leave Him all vengeance and/or justice

Many people want to forgive what the other person did, but they also want to pay back the person who did it to them. God tells us that we were not designed to handle bitterness and vengeance. (Romans 12:17-21; 13:4) It will eat us up inside and become a consuming way to live. It is only in letting go of the delivery of justice that we will be truly free to live our lives and reach our potential. There is a real need to tell God in prayer that we are turning over to Him and His authorized agents all vengeance and justice for the perpetrator. Therefore, tell God that He has total control over what happens to them in terms of punishment.

Dear Lord Jesus,

I give you full permission to handle any punishment or correction that may need to be done to _____. I thank you that you are an all-seeing God who is too holy to overlook sin and too loving to be needlessly cruel. I release _____ into your hands and release my mind, will, emotions, words, and actions from seeking my own pay-backs against _____. I will, Lord Jesus, for the security and safety of society participate in civil justice if this is needed to send a message or for justice to be served in a moral wrong.

In the Name of the Lord Jesus Christ,
Amen

Do this for each major offender in your life. The conversation with God around this prayer is important and liberating. The process of releasing the offender to God for His vengeance is not always easy. We must have an unshakable confidence in God's justice and in the fact that God knows all and saw the offense. It is possible that you may have this conversation with God a number of times because we all have a tendency to put ourselves back on vengeance patrol. But let God pursue the appropriate justice for the individual and get on with a great life that does not involve your offender or the memory of what they did.

1.

2.

3.

4.

5.

6.

7.

8.

9.

10.

Educate your offender about the consequences of their actions. Luke 19:21

The Scripture is clear that when someone sins against you, you have the right to educate them about the ways that they have sinned and the consequences of their selfishness. In the Bible this is called rebuking someone. We have come to see rebuke as scolding, yelling, or demeaning another person. But the main idea should be education. There needs to be an assumption that the person is not aware of all the ways that their actions, words, or attitudes have damaged others. Someone has to educate them. Yes, sometimes shame, and guilt are a part of the education process. I have seen many people make great strides when they educate their offender about what happened after the sin. It is important that this be done in a safe environment and when the offended party is emotionally and spiritually ready to do it. Many sinful and selfish people have never had anyone actually help them see their actions, words, and attitudes from the other person's perspective. It can be a significant growth step for a wounded person to confront their offender with what they did and what happened. This docs not have to be done, but there are many cases where this step of rebuking and educating your offender is important to letting it go. Who do you need to rebuke or educate?

1.

2.

3.

4.

5.

Make a list of the unintended consequences that have come from this offense so that you will be able to be accurate when you educate your offender. You may have a conversation that goes something like: "I wanted to have you know that I remember what you did to me. You were just being selfish, but your actions really damaged my life. When you did that to me, it caused these things to come into my life…"

1.

2.

3.

4.

5.

"All of these things are on you because of what you did. I am trusting God for the energy to move forward and beyond your sinfulness to me."

Release your offenders so you can experience the forgiveness of God. Matthew 6:14,15

There is a clear statement in the prayer that Jesus taught his disciples that talks about forgiveness. "Forgive us our trespasses as we forgive those who trespass against us." There is some connection between our willingness to let go of the offenses of others and our experience of the forgiveness of God. Therefore it is important that we make the conscious choice to release others to God for any vengeance and justice. We must let God and His agents pursue the justice that our offenders are due. Open your soul to the forgiveness of God by forgiving others. Go through those who have offended you and release them to God and invite His forgiveness into your heart.

I can distinctly remember a time when a woman came to apologize for the things she had done to hurt me. She was asking for forgiveness. I wanted to forgive her, but I heard myself saying, "No, I can't forgive you!" I was shocked with what I was saying. She had deeply hurt me, but I thought I could forgive her. But I could not. It was an incredibly awkward moment when the pastor could not forgive someone. I asked if I could pray. She agreed and I began to pour out my soul to God about how I knew I needed to forgive her but did not know how to do it. I pleaded with God to give me the ability to forgive her. I found myself praying out loud about all the things I was having difficulty forgiving her for. I went down a laundry list. Lord, I am having a hard time forgiving her for the time she did this... I am really not able to forgive her when she said this... I went on about 15-20 minutes in this way. All the while I was pleading with God for Him to give me His forgiveness for her. After about 20 minutes something happened. It was like a wave of the ocean just smashed into me from behind and I had a hard time staying seated on the coach. I felt God's forgiveness flood over me. Somewhere in the reciting what I felt she had done and somewhere in the pleading with God to allow me to forgive her, He released His forgiveness for her in my life. It was wonderful. At the of prayer, I looked her straight in the eye and told her from my heart that I forgave her.

Dear Jesus,

I release my offender to you for all punishment and justice. I will help your agents gain justice when it is needed, but I want your forgiveness of my sins to surround me and uphold me. I need your touch of grace in my life, so I leave to you the offenses of others.
In the Name of the Lord Jesus Christ,
Amen

P.S. If you have to tell God specifically what you are wanting to forgive them about, then spend time doing that. It really helped me.

Suffering to meet needs. 1 Peter 2:19-25.

In some instances of suffering the selfishness of another exposes their desperate need for something. At times God calls us to meet those needs exposed by the suffering in order to turn off the selfishness in the person's life. Just as Jesus suffered from our selfishness and condemnation "who for the joy set before Him endured the cross despised the shame and has sat down at the right hand of the throne of God" to meet our biggest need, which was the way back to God. The Apostle Peter tells us that at times Christians will be called upon to suffer so that right can be done; suffer so that one's selfishness can be stopped; suffer so that many can be saved. We have seen this kind of suffering for the greater good throughout the history of the church. Free men selling themselves into slavery in order to share the good news of Christ's forgiveness with those isolated away in slavery; Christians volunteering to be thrown to the lions to protect the Bible; men and women turning their backs on promising careers to serve the poor, the afflicted, and the oppressed; wives staying in marriages that produce deep wounds in them but staying for the good of the children. God does not call everyone to this kind and level of suffering but to some He does give this privilege. For most He calls us to a life of self-denial to show the grace and glory of Christ. Search the offense to see how many needs their offense represents which you could help heal.

Ask God if there are any parts of the suffering you have gone through, are going through, or may go through that can allow some greater righteous need or good to be accomplished. Ask Him for the grace to endure and the wisdom to remain righteous in the suffering. Let God know you are willing to be His instrument to bring healing and righteousness. As you think through your offenders, make a list of the needs that their offense highlights. Think through how you could righteously meet the need that is causing them to be sinfully selfish.

Do not be shallow if God is asking you to be deep. If God is asking you to stay in relationship with someone whom you can help heal, make sure that your staying is actually helping and not enabling the offender to keep offending. They are times when God asks us to bear the burdens of others, but we must do this with our eyes wide open.

Make a list of the needs that the other person's offense suggests. Can your suffering in any way be a way to heal that person?

1.

2.

3.

4.

5.

6.

7.

8.

9.

10.

Thank God and the offender for what the workouts did for you Luke 6:28

A number of times in my life God has prompted me to go back to those who offended me and thank them for how God has used them in my life to grow. This is never easy but it can be very releasing. I had the privilege of thanking a boss who was especially cruel. I had the privilege of thanking a person who did all they could to wreck my vocational career. I had the privilege of hugging one woman who was the instigator of the first split our church went through and I welcomed her back to the church.

Working through the various exercises in this chapter is designed to develop not just forgiveness but an active mercy that swallows up the hate, selfishness, and even evil of others in love. Biblical mercy is an active thing, and it wins by overwhelming evil with love. Jesus said to love your enemies and do good to those who despitefully use you. These are not empty words but marching orders for attacking with mercy. Jesus also tells us to bless those who curse us. This means that we tell the other person how what they did brought about a blessing or positive outcome in our life. If they were evil, then it is a rebuke to their evil, letting them know that they did not win but God won. If they were selfish, then it is a praise to God who can overrule the selfishness of another and turn it into a positive for you.

This often takes the other person off guard and can be an opportunity to allow your former tormentor to see Jesus in you. There is something powerful about gratefulness that flips the script of our power-hungry world. We are blessed when we allow active mercy to swallow the evil of others. We don't have to become best buddies with those who hurt us, but an insightful thank you can change you and lots of others.

Going the second mile. Matthew 5:38-42

Jesus tells us in the Sermon on the Mount that one of the ways to overcome bitterness is to invest more than is required in the person who is offending you. This is where Jesus says that if someone forces you to go one mile, go with him two miles. If someone sues you and wants to take your coat, give him your cloak also. We often try and give the least possible to those who have offended us and this, in some cases, keeps us bitter at our offender. Jesus tells us to become generous in our spirit towards the person and invest in them. I have found that if God wants you to make a second-mile investment in your offenders, He will let you know what your second-mile project is. It could be helping them in their business. It could be buying something from them. It could be paying more in alimony than is required. It could be talking nicely and politely. It could be recommending them for a job. It could be to give them some money. There are literally hundreds of different second-mile investments that God might suggest we make. Each of them is designed to break our bitterness and produce a generous spirit toward our offender.

What are some second-mile projects that God might have you pursue in order to free up your soul from demanding exact justice?

1.

2.

3.

4.

5.

Tell God that you will invest in a second-mile project to overcome their or your resentment.

Commit yourself to God beforehand so that if He prompts you with a second-mile project, you are already committed to doing it. One of the key ideas is that a second-mile investment is something beyond the common expected amount and displays a generous spirit and real love. Remember that second-mile projects never involve immorality or doing evil or violating any of God's clearly revealed will. Others might not completely agree with what God is telling you about a second-mile assignment, but it may be a crucial way to remove bitterness over a particular offender or offense. If you are prompted to do a second-mile project, share these promptings with a person who is wiser than you are and see if what you are talking about makes any sense to them.

Pray all the positive you can for this person.
Matthew 6:23-24

When someone offends us, we often can only focus on their mistakes and wrongs. We become so focused on the negative in their life that we cannot see the good or their needs. Unless we can change this single-minded focus on the bad, we will be unable to be free of their offense. One of the ways to do this is to pray positive into the lives of those who offend us. Jesus says to pray for those who persecute you, bless those who curse you, and love your enemies.

We want to break the negative emotional link between you and your offender by seeking to bless, pray, and love your enemy. See if you can help him/her succeed in a tangible way. One godly young woman I know found herself so troubled and bitter about some people at church that she began actually living out the verse *pray for those who persecute you*. She went up to each of her persecutors and asked if there were things she could pray about for them. She diligently prayed for these people and after a few months her heart had changed towards them. What are the positive things that you could pray for your offenders?

Offender:

1.
2.
3.
4.
5.

Dear Heavenly Father,

I right now today acknowledge my unforgiving heart, Lord Jesus, and I bow before you to release all my grudges, bitterness, and vengeance. I agree with you that I cannot become godly through bitterness. I have been held back in my Christian life. I seek to move forward, Lord Jesus, in intimacy with you and in service. Develop in me a forgiving spirit that is able to follow you regardless. I am asking you, blessed Holy Spirit, to cover me with your spirit for forgiveness and insight that I might be completely directed by you and walk as the blessed Lord Jesus Christ did, focused on the Father, ignoring the slights, offenses, and insults of those around Him. Lord Jesus, come and live your life again in me today that 1 might be free.

In the Name of the Lord Jesus Christ,

Amen

Secret #6

Purity of Heart

MATTHEW 5:8
Blessed are the pure in heart for they shall see God

6
Purity of Heart

Jesus said, "Blessed are pure in heart...." This beatitude is so incredibly profound that we are only now in the twentieth century beginning to understand its power. Let me explain. When I was growing up I tended to react to the world around me. If someone made me angry, I allowed myself to be angry. If I saw a pretty girl, I thought about that pretty girl. If I was presented with a choice, I often went with that choice. I never gave it a second thought that I should aim my mind at productive and beneficial things. I didn't know that I could control what my mind thought about and that this could make all the difference in my life. I let my mind, my will, and my emotions do what they wanted to do. In many cases it was not helpful.

My youth pastor, in the later years of high school, put a stop to my reactional way of living. He helped me enjoy the blessings of this beatitude even though I am not sure he knew that was what he was doing. He directed me into becoming a different person in a way I had never heard of before. He initiated biblical mental rehearsals. He gave me assignments to study Scripture, memorize Scripture, and meditate on Scripture. He repeatedly asked me to focus my mind on what Scripture said and then do it. He was filling my mind with purity and requiring that I live it out.

Let me give you a couple examples. One time we were talking and out of the blue he said, "I have been observing the way you relate to your family, and I don't

194

think you love your mother enough. I want you to memorize 1 Corinthians 13:4-8 and do what that passage says for your mother in whatever way God prompts you." Over the six months that he had me work on this assignment, it completely changed me and my relationship with my mother. I can remember another time he asked me if he heard right that I had a date with a particular girl. I said, "Yes, I did." He asked me to memorize 1 Thessalonians 4:1-8 and tell him exactly how the date was going to go minute by minute if I lived out that passage on that date. He would meet with me and listen to me recite the Scripture and then how that Scripture could be lived out in my life. He was asking me to pre-record myself living biblically before an event. He then had me play that movie in my head over and over until that is the way I acted when the actual event happened. My whole life began to change. I was beginning to mentally rehearse my life before it actually happened so I could be the best version of myself I could be. He would find an area of my life that was not what it should be and he would assign a passage of Scripture that told me how to correct that area. My youth pastor would make me go over and over Scripture about friends, lust, parents, anger, and ministry until I had mental movies of my doing each of those areas right. This made such a huge difference in my life.

Now with the advent of thirty years of findings in the area of positive psychology, we know that we can actually direct our mind towards positive, righteous, and good things. We can direct our minds rather than let them direct us. God has told us this fact in the Bible thousands of years ago, but we are only beginning to understand the scientific power behind what Jesus said. You and I can fill our minds with pure thoughts and mental movies of us behaving in the right way, and it will make a huge difference in the quality of our lives.

Most of us in the modern era are very familiar with mental rehearsal because of their use in sports. Ice skaters and most athletes now spend time visualizing their event thousands of times before they perform it live. The idea of mental practice is commonplace. What many of us don't realize is that this is what we can do with all of life. It can lead to dramatic improvements in your life and relationships. Imagine if before you get in a fight with your spouse, you mentally saw yourself living out James 1:19 "I am slow to speak, slow to anger and quick to listen." Imagine if you pre-recorded and mentally practiced saying and doing exactly the right thing in your interview or on your date or when faced with that person who irritates you. This is all possible.

You can actually mentally rehearse your life before it happens. You can take the truth of Scripture and inject it into your thinking and watch in your imagination your doing what God says in Scripture.

What if you took every problem area and memorized, mediated, and imagined yourself doing the biblical solution to that area? What if you were to mentally rehearse each of your encounters with others before you actually had the encounter? What if you took the time to mentally insert into your brain a motion picture of yourself acting exactly like the Bible said you should? What if you rehearsed that mental picture so many times that you actually acted just like the Bible suggested in real life? This is possible; in fact, it is what should happen. It is called spiritual growth.

Let me tell you that this is one of the secrets of blessed people. They have a pure and positive mind. Jesus said that the people who fill their mind with purity are blessed. Let me say it another way: The Happiest people think positive thoughts, make pure choices, and embrace righteous emotions. Let me help you see it from the negative side. Unhappy people think negative, cynical thoughts; make impure choices; and embrace dark, selfish emotions.

Joyful people think about positive things, not destructive or immoral things. It is very easy to focus on the problems, difficulties, and issues that we do not remember to work hard at filling our mind with that which is positive and pure. There is a lot in our world that is impure and immoral and destructive; but if our focus is on the negative, then we are excluded from certain blessings and a higher quality of life. When Jesus said that the people who are pure in their heart are blessed, He was right.

What is our heart?

Let's go deeper in what Jesus said. He said the pure in heart are blessed. What is the heart? That is equivalent of the soul. It is the real you. It is your mind, will, and emotions. The Bible tells us that we have a spirit, a soul, and a body. (1 Thessalonians 5:23) Our spirit is that place of our conscience, our connection to God, our personality, our creativity. Our soul is the place where we think, decide, and react to the world around us. It is what will be "beamed" out when we are taken to heaven. Our body is the actual hardware that God has contained all this software within. We will get a new body someday in heaven. (1 Corinthians 15:42-44)

197

Jesus is telling us that we can control what fills our soul. The blessings in life come from a pure, positive, loving soul and not a brooding, selfish, cynical soul. We seem to instinctively know this, but somehow we allow ourselves to be consumed with all the negative and twisted things around us. Jesus is calling us to a change in our soul: a focus on purity of the mind, will, and emotions.

Solomon wrote over 3,000 years ago, "Watch over your heart with all diligence, for from it flow the springs of life." Your heart is what you allow to constantly circulate in your mind, will, and emotions. Many of us have never stopped to consider that we actually can control what we constantly think about. It is essential that we do.

I have to admit that for years I came at this beatitude in the wrong way. For years every time I thought about purity of heart, I thought about removing impurity. I worked and strategized how to help people not think impure thoughts or do impure actions. But that approach ultimately won't work if that is your only strategy. Being less impure does not make you more pure. You have to fill your mind, will, and emotions with pure things, pure people, and pure situations. There is a place and an importance in removing impurity as long as you are increasing your purity. The last section of this chapter does spend time on removing impurity, but the focus of this chapter is how to have more purity.

Purity is a completely different element than impurity. Jesus says that the blessings come from having a purity of heart. Let's aim at filling our minds, will, and emotions with purity. It doesn't matter what you have done in the past, you can begin thinking, speaking, and acting in positive life-giving ways. It is down this path that a higher level of joy is waiting. You may have had lots of impure things happen to you. You may have participated in impure things. But you can decide today to begin to think about pure things and positive things. It is purity that is the way of joy, not impurity.

We are going to begin helping you form a pure mind – a mind that thinks about pure relationships, pure and positive images, pure and beneficial future dreams. This chapter will be the beginning of your journey to develop a pure and positive mental world. There are a number of biblical projects and exercises that can contribute to the development of purity of mind. I want to do for you what my youth pastor started in me so long ago. I want to help you grow in this essential quality of a pure soul.

There are two questions that the following exercises address:

1. How do you purify your soul?

2. How do you fill your soul with purity on a consistent basis?

Exercises for Developing Purity of Heart

Spiritual Disciplines

For over two thousand years people have practiced the spiritual disciplines to move them into the presence of God. When it comes to the issue of purity, there are three specific spiritual disciplines that address purity: Confession of Sin; Disciplines of Worship; Biblical Meditation. Let's take a look each of these in enough depth to allow you to do them.

Confession of Sin

In 1 John 1:9 Scripture declares that, "if we confess our sins, He is faithful and just to forgive us our sins and to cleanse us from all unrighteousness." This is quite a promise. The idea of confession is to agree with another about the issue. In this case it means to agree with God whether a particular action is right or wrong. When a person confesses they are agreeing with God's assessment about something.

Now it is important to understand two things about confession. First, it is based upon the work of Jesus Christ in His life, death, and resurrection. Jesus Christ lived a perfect life and voluntarily gave up that life so that His perfection could be substituted for your sins. He took your penalty and He took your sins. This is what makes confession work. There is nothing magical about agreeing with God that He is right and you were wrong when you did something He said not to do. But what makes your confession do anything is that Jesus Christ paid for your sins through His death on the cross which allows God to apply His payment to your sins.

When a person confesses to God that they are a sinner and incapable of getting to heaven on their own and in need of a Savior to be their perfection for them, they are becoming a Christian. Jesus Christ is the Savior of the World. All those who call on Him will be saved from the just punishment of God on sin. Therefore, if you have never prayed a prayer confessing your sin and inviting Jesus Christ to be your Savior then, let me suggest that you pray this prayer.

Dear Heavenly Father,

I realize that I am a sinner and incapable of earning your favor on my own. I have sinned against you and against others. I need a Savior. I right now invite Jesus Christ to be my Savior. I ask that all the forgiveness that is in Jesus Christ's death be applied to me. I ask you, Jesus Christ, to be my Savior and my Lord. Please come in and make me the kind of person you want me to be.

In the Name of the Lord Jesus Christ,
Amen

Jesus tells us in John 13:9,10 that we have a need for daily confession of sin as well as the major cleansing at salvation. Like the washing of feet to cleanse the dirt that was picked up during that day, so Christians need to let God cleanse them of the sins that they committed that day. Yes, these sins were covered by Christ's death on the cross, but Jesus asks us to let Him search us and see if there is any wicked way in us.

There are four ways that I have suggested that people do this. At the end of the day or during some quiet moment during the day go through a confession guide in prayer and let God interact with you about your specific sins for that day. I have also included a confession guide for dealing with sexual sins, since many associate impurity with sexual unfaithfulness.

The first confession guide is the seven deadly sins. This is the guide that was developed in the Middle Ages when the monks were asked which sins kill faith the most. They answered Pride, Envy, Anger, Lust, Sloth, Gluttony, and Greed. I recommend that you ask the Lord Jesus in prayer, "Have I committed any Pride today?" And pause and let God bring up any issues. Then ask, "Have I committed any Envy today?" Again you pause and let God bring things to mind. Then ask, "Have I committed any Anger today?" Again you pause and see if the Lord brings anything to mind. Go through all the seven deadly sins in like manner.

If the Lord brings anything to mind in any of the categories, then stop and confess that sin. Agree with God that that was wrong and ask Him to give you new ability to do something different the next time.

The second confession guide is the Ten Commandments. Go through each of the commandments and ask God if you have violated the letter or the spirit of that command. Martin Luther and other Christians down through the centuries have used the Ten Commandments as their confession guide. If the Lord brings anything up, then confess what you did wrong to Him and ask Him to apply that sin to the work of Christ on the cross. Change your mind about that sin and ask for His energy to not commit it the next time the opportunity arises.

The third confession guide that many have found helpful is the three-type-of-sins list. These are Sins of Omission, Sins of Commission, and Wickedness. Ask God, "Have I committed any sins of Omission today?" Pause and let God bring anything to mind you failed to do. Confess that sin, make plans to fix what you did, and ask God for energy to not make that mistake the next time. Then move on to asking God, "Have I committed any Sins of Commission today?" Again pause and let God bring things to your mind. If He does, then confess and repent of those actions being very thankful for all that God has provided in the death of Christ. Finally, ask God, "Have I committed any Wickedness today?" Let God guide you to a place of healing and forgiveness from any wrong actions you participated in.

The fourth confession guide is to ask God if you have committed any selfishness in any of the ten relationships of your life. In this confession guide you would start in prayer and ask God if you have been selfish in your relationship with Him. Pause and let God show you any ways this has been true. Then move through the rest of the relationships of your life: Personal life, Marriage/Dating, Family, Work, Finances, Church, Friends, Enemies, Society.

This is a lost discipline these days to cleanse our lives every day through confession of the sins For further information on these disciplines, please look at the chapter on Confession in my book *Spiritual Disciplines of a C.H.R.I.S.T.I.A.N.*

Confessing your sexual sins: 1 John 1:9; Matthew 5:11

Because of the enduring nature of sexual impurity, let me add a confession guide from just the area of physical intimacy. This not the only kind of impurity that is possible, but it is often very helpful for people to comb through their sexual lives with the Lord and specifically receive His forgiveness in this area. Listed below are the sexual sins that are destructive to a healthy marriage, family, and individual. Look at the list and pray a prayer of confession for the sins that you have been involved in. If you do not know about something on the list, do not worry about that one.

- Pornography: Leviticus 18:6-18
- Mental adultery: Matthew 5:28
- Transvestitism (Cross-Dressing): Deuteronomy 22:5
- Physical defrauding during dating: Galatians 5:19
- Masturbation: Galatians 5:19, Romans 1:20-31
- Pre-Marital episodes: Deuteronomy 22:22-29
- Adultery: Leviticus 20:10-12, Deuteronomy 22:22
- Prostitution: Deuteronomy 22:17-18
- Indecent exposure, voyeurism: Deut. 22:17-18
- Homosexual episodes: Leviticus 18:22,20:13
- Incest: Leviticus 18:6-18, 20:14
- Bestiality: Leviticus 18:23, 20:15,16
- Spiritual sexual episodes: Genesis 6:3; Jude 1:6
- Necrophilia: Numbers 19:13
- Sacrificial sexuality: Leviticus 18:21; 20:6; Deut. 19:14

Pray the prayer of confession about each of your sins. Remember, there is forgiveness in Jesus the Christ. He is not waiting to condemn but to comfort and forgive.

Dear Lord Jesus,

I agree with You that _____ is wrong. I turn away from it and ask that all the forgiveness that is in your death on Calvary be applied to my sin in this area. I realize that only in your power and energy and through your direction can I successfully turn away from this sin. Thank you, Lord Jesus, for dying on the Cross for me. I choose to cooperate with you in _____ area of my life so that the process you began in me when I first trusted in You can continue. (Philippians 1:6).

I repudiate, reject, and renounce any ground, place, or power I may have given to Satan in my life through my involvement in _____. I give to the Lord Jesus Christ all power over this area of my life. I surrender this area to the Lord Jesus Christ and the Holy Spirit. I ask you, Lord Jesus, that you would fill this area of my life with the Holy Spirit of truth, so that I would be wise, thankful, and able to see your plan in this area in the future.

I cancel any contract I may have made with Satan through _____. I ask you, Lord Jesus, to cleanse me of any and all unrighteousness (including demons and demonic strongholds) because you say in your Word in 1 John 1:9 that "if we confess our sins He is faithful and just to forgive us our sins and to cleanse us of all unrighteousness."

In the Name and for the Glory of the Lord Jesus Christ, Amen

205

The Spiritual Discipline of Worship

Another one of the spiritual disciplines that will fill us with purity of heart is the discipline of Worship. There is something amazing that happens when we take time personally or with others and give praise, adoration, thanksgiving, and pre-eminence to God Almighty. This also can be a daily discipline. Set aside five to thirty minutes each day and thank God for who He is, what He has done, and what you hope He will do. I have suggested that people take time at every meal to thank God for at least three things about their life. I have suggested that people spend time adoring God for His Essence, Attributes, Nature, Names and/or Great Works. Because this discipline is so profitable I have written a book that takes a person on a forty-day journey of praise through the five essential aspects of God's being. The book is called *Touching the Face of God.*

The Spiritual Discipline of Biblical Meditation

The Bible promises huge benefits to those who will meditate on the Scriptures and thereby fill their mind with the thoughts and concepts of God. (Joshua 1:8; Psalm 1:1-3; Colossians 3:15,16) There is much confusion over meditation these days because most of what we hear about meditation comes from eastern meditation. Eastern meditation is the desire to empty the mind so that it goes blank and something from the "other world" can then fill it. This is not the kind of meditation that the Scripture tells us to do. Biblical Meditation is filling the mind with the verses, phrases, and ideas from the Bible so that your mind is then changed around those concepts. Technically Biblical

Meditation is pressing the Bible through our mind, will, emotions, and body so that it becomes a part of who we are. There are a number of techniques that we see in the Bible for injecting the Bible into us. I want to focus on only five of eleven different Biblical Meditation techniques: Slow Repetition, Bible Study, Personalize, Visualize, and Praying. Just as my youth pastor changed my life with biblical mental rehearsals I want to help you gain all the benefits of this beatitude through Biblical Meditation.

Slow Repetition

When I became a Christian, a man challenged me to slowly repeat the Scriptures out loud under my breath as I went to sleep. I began doing this simple exercise and saw amazing things began to happen in my life. God has blessed me in numerous ways: relationally, vocationally, financially, and spiritually because of my regular practice of Biblical Meditation. God has been extremely gracious to me over the years as an answer to His promises on Biblical Meditation.

Take whatever verse of Scripture that you know by heart or are interested in studying and repeat it out loud as you are going to bed. Emphasize different words. Think about the concepts, ideas, and results of the verse. Picture yourself living out the truth of the verse. Act on the information in the verse. This simple practice will change your life.

If you do not have any verses that come to mind, then start with the verses that I started with – Psalm 1:1-3.

Just say it slowly over and over again until you fall asleep. Let the truths sink into your soul.

When I was just getting started, my youth pastor would assign verses that he thought I needed. Now, when I realize that I need to grow in an area, I will look up verses on that topic and meditate on them so that I will begin to act differently.

You may be saying right now that you don't have time to add anything else to your schedule. But you do have time to repeat Scripture as you are going to bed. If you are not careful, you will only be meditating on the news stories or television programs you watched before you went to bed. Do something constructive and slowly repeat Scripture as you go to bed.

What started out as reciting a Bible verse as I was falling asleep has become a lifelong habit of Biblical Meditation and Bible study. I cannot recommend any spiritual exercise more than this one. Throughout Scripture there are promises and evidence of what happens when a person injects their mind with the Scriptures. The Bible tells us that if we mediate upon the words and phrases of the Scripture, God will do some amazing things for us. Listen to the Scriptures:

Joshua 1:8
*This book of the law shall not depart from your mouth, but you shall meditate on it day and night, so that you may be careful to do according to all that is written in it; **for then you will make your way prosperous, and then you will have success.***

Psalms 1:1-3
How blessed is the man who does not walk in the counsel of the wicked, Nor stand in the path of sinners, Nor sit in the seat of scoffers! But his delight is in the law of the LORD, And in His law he meditates day and night. <u>He will be like a tree firmly planted by streams of water, Which yields its fruit in its season And its leaf does not wither; And in whatever he does, he prospers.</u>

Colossians 3:15,16
Let the word of Christ richly dwell within you, with all wisdom teaching and admonishing one another with psalms and hymns and spiritual songs, <u>singing with thankfulness in your hearts to God.</u>

Bible Study

One of the key Biblical Meditation techniques is Bible Study. Dig beneath the surface of text and let God speak from the richness of the Bible. There is a standard way to study the Scriptures: Observe a passage by reading it out loud three times, writing it on a separate sheet of paper in some diagrammatical form, circle the key words or phrases, write down the questions that come to mind when you are reading this passage, note the transitions, and compare other translations.

Now you are ready to interpret what the passage is really saying: Define the key words by looking them up in a dictionary; check the cross references; look at background information in a Bible dictionary or Bible Encyclopedia; look at some commentaries to make sure you haven't embraced a heretical view; and write your own personal translation that brings the power of Scripture to light.

Finally you are ready to apply the Scriptures to your life now that you have observed it and interpreted it properly. For each Scripture you study, God has something that He wants you to know, feel, or do because of that Scripture. You should ask God what it is that He wants you do know, feel, or do and write down these action steps and begin doing them.

Personalize

To personalize Scripture is to write or speak your name, your sins, your temptations, your circumstances, your problems, your situations, your concerns, etc., into the passage. The process of inserting your name and your issues into Scriptures as you read or write the Scriptures often is very emotional. I will often have people write out Romans 6:1-23, Romans 8:1-17 or James 1:2-5 with their name or sins inserted and watch them feel the power of God touching, speaking, and empowering them.

Visualize

Biblical mental rehearsal is one of the most powerful concepts in all of literature. Modern science is only now understanding that the brain automatically moves us toward what we regularly visualize. There are three different modes of visualizing Scripture. Let me walk you through each one.

To visualize the Scriptures means:

1. To Picture yourself doing the Biblical Truth – Actions, Reactions, Words, Thoughts, Attitudes, Motives The idea here is to make a mental movie of yourself actually doing what the Bible says. The more vivid and real your mental rehearsal, the more you will act this way in real life. If you cannot see yourself acting in a biblical way in your head, then you will never act this way in real life. All of us would like to be calmer, wiser, less prone to lust, pride, or anger; but that will not happen until you see yourself being that way in your mind first. Understand what God wants and then see yourself doing it in your mind and it will show up in your actual behavior.

Let me give you a few exercises for you to work through:

James 1:19 *But everyone must be quick to hear, slow to speak and slow to anger.* Mentally put yourself in situations that would occur in your normal week: a time with a boss or irritating driver or co-worker or spouse. Replay the events of the past with your behaving in this new way that is based upon James 1:19. Instead of smart-mouthing back, you listen more deeply to their point. Instead of talking so much, you just go silent. Instead of powering up in anger, see yourself just going calm and relaxed. It may take a few times before you can even successfully see yourself behaving this way in your mind. But it is essential that you actually play out the various scenarios with your being quick to hear, slow to speak, and slow to anger. Once you do this, then it will begin and then this new behavior will "magically" begin to appear in your life.

The Fruit of the Spirit. If we are going to start allowing the Spirit of the Living God to pour through us, then we have to have a clear mental picture of what that looks like in your life. Galatians 5:22,23 says ...*the fruit of the spirit is love, joy, peace, patience, kindness, goodness, gentleness, faithfulness and self-control; against such things there is no law.* The following is an expanded understanding of the fruit of the spirit. Read through this list three times each day. See yourself letting God do these actions through you. If you keep repeating these ideas each morning – seeing yourself doing them – you will begin to see the Holy Spirit show up and do these in your life.

Love: I am alert every day to God's impulses to meet someone's needs, to pursue their soul, and/or to please them in some way.

Joy: I am sensitive to the prompting of God to deepen my relationships and be positive with others.

Peace: I stop making war needlessly with others and find a way to be in harmony with others if possible.

Patience: I constantly draw upon God's power to keep persevering toward a righteous goal.

Kindness: I am alert to how I can adjust my interactions to be more pleasant, merciful, and encouraging.

Goodness: I listen hard for God's specific ways of benefitting others.

Meekness: I am flexible and calm when my expectation are not met, and I make thoughtful requests and wise adaptations.

Faithfulness: I am alert to the Lord's promptings to trust Him and stay the righteous course.

Self-Control: I am sensitive to the Holy Spirit as He seeks to moderate my desires.

Put a copy of this list on the bathroom mirror or on your phone or laminate a copy and put it in the shower. There is great value in saying these out loud, picturing yourself doing these.

The Beatitudes: If we are going to start allowing the Spirit of the Living God to pour through us then we have to have a clear mental picture of what that looks like in your life. Matthew 5:3-12 tells us the Beatitudes. It is the basis of this whole book, but it is also another way that the Holy Spirit wants to flow through us. The following is a succinct understanding of the Beatitudes so that you can actually see what it looks like to let God's spirit do this through you. Read through this list three times per day. If you keep repeating these ideas each morning – seeing yourself doing them – you will begin to see the Holy Spirit show up and do these in your life. Just saying these over and over again will give you a mental picture that can grasp when God is trying to prompt you to move in these directions. See yourself acting like this.

Blessed are the poor in spirit for theirs is the kingdom of heaven: I am aware of how I need God and others. I am teachable and I do not need to be the center of attention.

213

Blessed are those who mourn for they shall be comforted: I do not make excuses or cover up my failures and shortcomings, and I take the time to grieve the losses and pain in my life.

Blessed are the meek for they shall inherit the earth: I am flexible and calm when my expectations are not met and I make thoughtful requests and wise adaptations.

Blessed are those who hunger and thirst after righteousness for they shall be satisfied: I have a burning desire to see the right things done, and I know the righteous cause(s) God wants me to promote.

Blessed are the merciful for they shall receive mercy: I forgive others, look for second-mile opportunities to overcome feelings of bitterness, and hand all vengeance to God.

Blessed are the pure in heart for they shall see God: I make sure that my core thoughts, choices, and emotions are pure and positive.

Blessed are the peacemakers for they shall be called the sons of God: I inject calm and harmony wherever I go. I help others stop creating war with each other. I restore people's relationships with God and the key people in their life.

Blessed are those who have been persecuted for righteousness for theirs is the kingdom of heaven: I stand up for what is right even if it is inconvenient and costly.

Blessed are you when men revile you and persecute you and say all manner of evil against you falsely on account of Me. I openly identify with Jesus even if it brings insults and hatred.

Put a copy of this list on the bathroom mirror or on your phone or laminate a copy and put it in the shower. There is great value in saying these out loud, picturing yourself doing these.

Sexual Purity: This is the actual list of verses that my youth pastor put me through when he began to work on sexual purity with me. I had to memorize each one of these passages and describe in detail how it would look for me to live out these concepts and ideas. I can remember going through all eleven different Biblical Meditation techniques for each of these verses. These meditation exercises were hugely responsible for allowing me to remain sexually pure until marriage.

- 1 Corinthians 3:13 *each man's work will become evident; for the day will show it because it is to be revealed with fire, and the fire itself will test the quality of each man's work.*

- 2 Corinthians 10:3-5 *For though we walk in the flesh, we do not war according to the flesh, for the weapons of our warfare are not of the flesh, but divinely powerful for the destruction of fortresses. We are destroying speculations and every lofty thing raised up against the knowledge of God, and we are taking every thought captive to the obedience of Christ.*

215

- James 1:2-4 *Consider it all joy, my brethren, when you encounter various trials, knowing that the testing of your faith produces endurance. And let endurance have its perfect result, so that you may be perfect and complete, lacking in nothing.*

- 1 Thessalonians 4:3-5 *For this is the will of God, your sanctification; that is, that you abstain from sexual immorality; that each of you know how to possess his own vessel in sanctification and honor, not in lustful passion, like the Gentiles who do not know God.*

- Romans 6:11-13 *Even so consider yourselves dead to sin but alive to God in Christ Jesus. Therefore do not let sin reign in your mortal body so that you obey its lusts, and do not go on presenting the members of your body to sin as instruments of unrighteousness; but present yourselves to God as those alive from the dead, and your members as instruments of righteousness to God.*

- Galatians 5:16 *But I say, walk by the Spirit, and you will not carry out the desire of the flesh.*

- Galatians 5:22,23 *But the fruit of the Spirit is love, joy, peace, patience, kindness, goodness, faithfulness, gentleness, self-control; against such things there is no law.*

- Galatians 5:24 *Now those who belong to Christ Jesus have crucified the flesh with its passions and desires.*

- Colossians 3:2,5 *Set your mind on the things above, not on the things that are on earth. Therefore consider the members of your earthly body as dead to immorality, impurity, passion, evil desire, and greed, which amounts to idolatry.*

- Hebrews 12:11,12 *All discipline for the moment seems not to be joyful, but sorrowful; yet to those who have been trained by it, afterwards it yields the peaceful fruit of righteousness. Therefore, strengthen the hands that are weak and the knees that are feeble.*

- Psalms 1:1-3 *How blessed is the man who does not walk in the counsel of the wicked, Nor stand in the path of sinners, Nor sit in the seat of scoffers! But his delight is in the law of the Lord, and in His law he meditates day and night. He will be like a tree firmly planted by streams of water, which yields its fruit in its season and its leaf does not wither; and in whatever he does, he prospers.*

- Proverbs 15:3 *The eyes of the Lord are in every place, watching both the evil and the good.*

- Psalms 119:9,11 *How can a young man keep his way pure? By keeping it according to Your word. Your word I have treasured in my heart, That I may not sin against You.*

- Judges 16:21 *Then the Philistines seized him and gouged out his eyes; and they brought him down to Gaza and bound him with bronze chains, and he was a grinder in the prison.*

  - Psalms 19:14 *Let the words of my mouth and the meditation of my heart be acceptable in Your sight, O Lord, my rock and my Redeemer.*

  - Job 31:1 *I have made a covenant with my eyes; How then could I gaze at a virgin?*

  - Romans 12:1,2 *Therefore I urge you, brethren, by the mercies of God, to present your bodies a living and holy sacrifice, acceptable to God, which is your spiritual service of worship. And do not be conformed to this world, but be transformed by the renewing of your mind, so that you may prove what the will of God is, that which is good and acceptable and perfect.*

As I have said, I was blessed as a young man by a youth pastor who made me mentally rehearse being different in a biblical way. God literally changed my life through his mental rehearsal sessions. I cannot recommend this exercise enough. In any area where you are struggling or where you know there is more you can learn, begin to visualize yourself living out the biblical truth in that area.

2. To picture the Biblical Scene – Sights, sounds, smells, touch, taste.

This is where you read the passage and even study the passage so that you can make an accurate mental movie of the scene. What do things look like? What do things smell like?

What is the texture of the fabric and the day? What is the general impression that the whole scene gives off? Actually make the mental movie of this scene from the Bible.

Down through the centuries Christians have been making these kinds of mental movies and have been hugely strengthened in their faith when they face similar situations and challenges. This is where you watch the miracle take place. You see the disciples talk back to Jesus.

3. To picture yourself in the Biblical Scene – Five senses and Asking, Interacting, Reacting

This is a slight variation on the exercise above, but you put yourself in the scene as one of the participants. In the previous situation you studied it and observed it from an invisible overview position. In this mental rehearsal you are the little boy handing the five loaves and two fish to Jesus. You are one of the disciples who sees Jesus begin to rise above your heads and then vanish into heaven. You are Sampson's mother who hears the angel tell you that this boy will be a Nazarite from birth. You are one of the disciples of Jesus listening as he explains the mysteries of the kingdom of God.

When you inject yourself into the actual scene as one of the characters in it, then you will look around at what is happening – smell the smells, feel the press of the crowd, look deep into the eyes of Jesus. Your engagement in the story will bring out new emotions and new interactions with God.

Pray

Another very powerful form of Biblical Meditation is to pray the Scripture back to God. Ask for everything that is possible in the passage. One of the things that God takes delight in is when His children ask Him for what He has already said He wants to give them. Open to any passage and read it a few times, then start asking God for what is good and righteous in that passage.

Biblical Meditation is such an important and neglected spiritual discipline that I wrote a whole book on just how to meditate on the Bible: *They Laughed When I Wrote Another Book About Prayer.* In this book I detail eleven different ways to meditate on the Bible and see its benefits flow into your life.

Righteous Idealization

Describe a healthy, positive, pure life five years in the future

If you are going to utilize the grace of God to build and enjoy a pure life, then you must know what that life looks like. Olympic athletes decide that they want to be Olympians and what it will look and feel like to experience that achievement. They think of the skills, times, scores, and accomplishments that they will need to achieve to become an Olympian. Then they eliminate the things that will not let them get to those places. In the same way, if you want the blessing of God, the peace of God, and the healthy relationships that God promises, you must go after these positive, pure goals and eliminate what will keep you from getting there. It is not as hard to eliminate something you like doing if you know what you want to accomplish. Go for purity; it is worth it.

Let's picture a time five years in the future in which your life is positive, pure, and deeply enjoyable. There is something amazing that happens when we picture the ideal future and begin to detail it out. It is like a prayer. If we think about it every day, then God and you begin to move toward that ideal future – what is happening and what are you thinking and doing. Let's look at a few of the key areas of your life.

What does the ideal positive, pure future look like five years from now? Detail out the following areas. If my life were ideal five years from now in these areas, what would it be like? Activities, Weight, Finances, Friends, Sleep, Job, Marriage, Family, Spirituality.

This exercise was one of the most life-changing exercises I have ever done. I have done it repeatedly through my life, and it never ceases to amaze me how it moves me to another level when I do this. I will often spend two and three months doing this exercise every night for a half hour or so.

If my marriage or romantic life were ideal, what would it look like in five years? Describe it in detail.

If my job or career were ideal in five years, what would I be doing and where? Describe it in detail.

If my finances were ideal in five years, what would I be earning? What would I be saving? What would I be giving? And to whom? Describe this in detail.

If my personal life were ideal in five years, what would it be like? Describe it in detail?

Developing Role Models and Mentors

It is important to know what purity looks and feels like. We often learn far more about what we really want in life from watching people who are doing it well. Without mentors and role models, it is much harder to grasp life-giving purity. Who are your mentors in each of the key relationships? If you don't have any role models in an area, then that may be an area of great struggle because you have no one to show you how it is done. Don't be afraid to ask people to be your mentors or role models.

Who are your role models for your spirituality and your relationship with God?

Who are your role models for personal development success and a maximized life?

Who are your role models for a great marriage?

Who are your role models for a great and enjoyable family life?

Making Life-Giving Movies In Your Head. Phil. 4:8

The Scriptures are clear that we are to reject evil, impure, and damaging thoughts and images; but we can only reject them if we have something more powerful and compelling to think about instead. Notice that the Scriptures say in Philippians 4:8 *whatever is true, whatever is honorable, whatever is right, whatever is pure, whatever is lovely, whatever is of good repute, if there is any excellence and if anything worthy of praise, think* on these things.

When temptation comes at us, we need to be prepared with mental images of great times with our spouse, deeply joyful times with our children, exciting righteous times having fun, encouraging times of success and achievement, or overwhelming times with the Lord. If we have not had these memories, then make movies of these times about the future. When it is time to say no to temptation, we must say yes to great movies of righteous pure things.

When you are bored or depressed or anxious, you can chose to pull the destructive movie down from the shelf (porn, depressive, horror, blasphemous) or put on the encouraging film. Your mind works the same way... Decide what movie you will put on when temptation is prompting you.

List the great times of the past. I try and take pictures of all the good times so that I can have the pictures come up as screen savers on my computer. In this way I am always reminded of the positive and pure times in my life. I find that if I don't have the pictures, I can forget about really good times from the past.

Another way to have positive pure life-giving movies is to make new ones with your loved ones all the time. Plan something fun, exciting, and positive every month. If you are not a good planner, then join a church group or organization that has activities and projects that will be memorable for you. If we have things to look forward to, then we will have a way of pushing out the impure as we focus on the pure.

Make a list of activities and events you would like to go to that are positive. There are lots of different things to do if you actually sit down and list them. Now just put them in the calendar.

When you are tempted, you must have positive images and ideas to think about instead of tempting ones. What are your most positive memories and ideas in each of these areas? Force your mind to dwell on delightful ideas and memories so that you will not be thinking about the temptation.

There is an amazing joy and liberation in purity. Purity is about thinking, speaking, and acting in a positive life-giving way. Purity means that a person does not mix their thoughts, speech, or actions with destructive or selfish ways. Purity is being truly beneficial to yourself, others, and society. Purity is not always what we want, but it is what we need. Deep inside we want people to look out for our good and not just their selfish advantage. Purity reenergizes and restores. Too often in Christian circles we think of purity in terms of what it is not. But sometimes this causes us to focus on the impure.

A pure action is one which honors God, benefits others, and ourselves. When we add something that is destructive, self-serving, or manipulative, it becomes impure. Becoming pure is not about saying no as much as it is about saying yes to healthy relationships, yes to life-giving thoughts, yes to benefiting others, yes to deep intimacy with God, yes to soul-enriching activities, yes to restorative community projects. It is almost impossible to win against impurity by focusing on saying NO. To really embrace purity, one must focus on what should be done, what should be said, and what should be thought. Eliminate what is toxic, draining, and poisonous to your life and relationships but don't put the focus there.

The question becomes: How can I increase my enjoyment of life, marriage, and family without doing things that will harm them or the relationship itself? Could a person put the energy, time, and money they are spending on destructive activities into positive and pure things?

There is purity all around us, but impurity is screaming at us so that we will not see the purity that is so much better for us. Make no mistake; there are toxic elements in our society that will destroy the individual, marriages, families, and even communities. The usual impure suspects are alcohol, drugs, prostitution, gambling, pornography, and the like. These impure actions promise immediate pleasure, hoping you will forget the consequences that are coming down the road.

Remove Hidden Provisions for Defeat: Romans 13:14

When the ancient Greeks landed on an enemy shore, they motivated their army to go forward by burning the boats they had just arrived on. Imagine the motivation that this image presented to the army. The only way to stay alive was to defeat the army in front of you. There was no retreat. Many times we leave ways of giving into temptation because we really want to fall back into those ways again. I have watched alcoholics hide a bottle of vodka in the toilet tank. I have watched people who are committed to losing weight hide Oreo cookies in the linen closet, so in case they are desperate they will be able to find some food. I had a man who took all the pornography from his home when I told him to remove it. But he put it in his truck because it was worth so much, and he didn't really want to part with it. There is a part of us that is very drawn to particular temptations and sins that we have committed in the past. We often allow ourselves vulnerable places where we could fall into temptation and sin because we really want to. If we are going to be honest with God and ourselves, we must eliminate all of these hidden provisions for sin. Only you know what and where they all are. If you are serious, you must remove these.

What provisions have you left in your life that allow you to give into temptation?

Images, Movies, Pornography, Relationships, Reminders, Equipment

Get a handle on the influences in your life

If we are ever going to reach our maximal potential and succeed as God would have us, we must come to grips with the principle of influence. We are in large measure the product influences that have been or are a part of our lives. We have control over many of those influences. If we choose wisely, then we will be propelled toward wisdom and righteousness. If we choose poorly or not at all, then we will be driven to wickedness and folly. If you want to get a firm grip on doing something with your life and becoming successful, then understand and work with the principle of influence. We must live in the real world, not the one we want to live in or the one that people have said is real. It is not true when you say, "Oh, that does not affect me." You may not be aware of how it affects you. You may not be as much affected by that as someone else. You may be affected in a positive way. However, you are still affected.

We must open our eyes to see that all things exert an influence on our lives and should be examined in terms of what type of influence they exert. We must realize that every day of our lives is a battle for our minds because:

EVERYTHING INFLUENCES YOU!!!!
EVERY PERSON,
EVERY CHOICE,
EVERY MEMORY,
EVERY SITUATION

EVERYTHING INFLUENCES YOU EITHER
TOWARD GOOD OR EVIL,
WISDOM OR FOLLY.

We do not have a choice whether something will influence us; we only have a choice whether to allow that thing into our lives to exert its influence. The more we surround ourselves with positive influences, the more we will please God in all we think, say, and do.

Read what the Scripture says about influences:

- Matthew 5:29,30 *If your right eye makes you stumble, tear it out, and throw it from you; for it is better for you that one of the parts of your body perish, than for your whole body to be thrown into hell. And if your right hand makes you stumble, cut if off and throw if from you; for it is better for you that one of the parts of your body perish, than for your whole body to go into hell.*

- 1 Corinthians 15:33 *Do not be deceived; bad company corrupts good morals.*

- Philippians 4:8 *Finally, brethren, whatever is true, whatever is honorable, whatever is right, whatever is pure, whatever is lovely, whatever is of good repute, if there is anything worthy of praise, let your mind dwell on these things.*

- 2 Timothy 2:22 *Run away from anything that gives you the evil thoughts that young men often have, but stay close to anything that makes you want to do right. Have faith and love, and enjoy the companionship of those who love the Lord and have pure hearts.*

- 2 Timothy 3:6 *For among them are those who enter into households and captivate weak women weighed down with sins, led on by various impulses.*

- 2 Peter 2:7 *And if He rescued righteous Lot, oppressed by the sensual conduct of unprincipled men (for by what he saw and heard that righteous man, while living among them, felt his righteous soul tormented day after day with their lawless deeds), then the Lord knows how to rescue the godly from temptation, and to keep the unrighteous under punishment for the day of judgment.*

Some things, some people, and\or some situations influence us to hate, some to love, some to lust, some to anger, some to peace, some to discipline, some to laziness. Each person reacts differently to each influence, but each person is influenced by everything. When a person sees a forest, a movie, hears an orchestra or a heavy metal concert, it all influences for good or bad. It may only exert a mild influence on a person, but it exerts an influence. If we are to present ourselves to God as an acceptable sacrifice, we must get a handle on the influences of our lives.

How to Get a Handle on the Influences of My Life

1. Realize that influences are judged by their effects or results.

This means that it is NOT possible to tell whether a particular thing is a good or a bad thing just by deciding whether I want to do it or whether a lot of other people are doing it. This means that something is not necessarily a good thing just because it makes me feel good in the present (drugs, alcohol, affairs, cheating). All influences must be judged by their ultimate effect or result in my life.

What are the evil, unrighteous, harmful, or foolish things that I am doing or want to do?

Evil / Foolish Activities	Influences

229

Evil / Foolish Activities	Influences

It is sometimes more helpful to let someone close to you (who you can trust) fill out the things that are foolish, unrighteous, harmful, or evil. What are the influences that are encouraging these activities? Put down an influence even if it is not the total cause of the activity.

2. Learn what produces negative results in your life.

One of the most interesting ways to track the influences in your life is to look at the things that are evil and ask what makes you think or act in that direction. Sometimes it is an activity that most people don't think is wrong; but for you that activity, show, book, or magazine produces the beginnings of evil. Ask yourself what makes you think, act, or speak in a destructive direction. If you are honest, you will be surprised.

What makes me think, act, and speak with the evil mentioned in Romans 1:29-31?

Greed, Malice, Envy, Murderous intentions, Strife, Deceit, Gossip, Slander, Hatred toward God, Insolence, Arrogance, Boastful, Evil, Disobedience to parents, Disloyalty, Unloving spirit, a Lack of mercy

What makes me think, act, and speak with the evil mentioned in Galatians 5:19 ?

> Immoral, Impure, Sensual, Idolatrous, Superstitious, Vengeful, Spiteful, Jealous, Explosive with anger, Argumentative, Disagreeable, Factious, Envious, Drunken, Carousing

What makes me think, act, and speak with the evil mentioned in 1 Peter 4:3?

> Unnecessarily sexual, Unable to contain my bodily appetites, Intoxicated and out of control, Carousing, Wild (Party-goer), Accepting of false religions

3. Learn what influences you to be more pleasing to God.

In the same way that we can only tell whether something is unfavorable by what it pushes us toward in the long run, so we can only tell about the good influences in our lives by examining what the activities make us do in the long run. This is another case in which it is best to let someone else point out your positive points. What are the influences that tend to push me toward these positive things? Put them next to the activity.

What things make me think, speak, and act with the positive and pure qualities mentioned in Galatians 5:22, 23?

> Loving, Joyful, Peaceful, Patient, Kind, Meek, Faithful, Self-Controlled

What things make me think, speak, and act with the positive and pure qualities mentioned in Philippians 4:8?

> Truthful, Mannered, Respectful,
> Humble, Righteous, Pure, Pleasant,
> Lovely, Wise, Excellent, Filled with
> Praise

4. Ruthlessly substitute the positive for the negative.

Jesus said, *If your right hand causes you to stumble cut it off and throw it from you. If your right eye causes you to stumble cut it out and throw if from you.* Matthew 5:29,30

Jesus is not interested in one-eyed or one-armed Christians. He wants us to remove the people, circumstances, situations, and activities that produce sin, selfishness, and evil in our life. Some people find that certain kinds of music trigger them to wanting to get drunk or be promiscuous. Others find that when they go to certain kinds of gatherings or events, they are "encouraged" to remember their days of wild behavior. Whenever you find a negative behavior or influence, you need to find something positive to put in its place. It is not helpful to just tell yourself you won't do those things. We will never conquer our temptations and bad habits until we are willing to substitute a positive action, idea, or practice for a negative one. It is not enough to just say that we will no longer do the negative. If we do not put a positive practice in its place, then a vacuum is created; and we will go back to thinking about the evil influence or action.

Colossians 3:5,12 *Therefore consider the members of your earthly body as dead to immorality, impurity, passion, evil desire, and greed, which amounts to idolatry... And so, as those who have been chosen of God, holy and beloved, put on a heart of compassion, kindness, humility, gentleness, and patience...*

Are there things in your life that may be okay for other people but not for you because they consistently influence you to act in ways that are destructive to others or to yourself?

1.

2.

3.

4.

5.

Secret #7

Peacemakers

Matthew 5:10
Blessed are the peacemakers
for they shall be called the Sons of God

7
Peacemakers

How do I inject peace into the tension in my life?

Most people are used to thinking about making peace by having more power. If I have more power than the other person, then they have to do it my way. Many attempts at peacemaking in marriage counseling, work relations, and financial dealings involve lawyers, judges, police, and establishing positions of power. I actually find that many people will want me to do marriage counseling with them only to confirm that they are right and that their spouse should admit it. Peace through power is not the kind of peace that Jesus is directing us to pursue here. Now there are times to establish détente through power so that you can actually pursue peace. But real peace is much deeper and more rewarding than power.

The word *peace* means the cessation of war and living in harmony. Therefore whenever there is tension, one of two things are true: 1) there is active war taking place or 2) there is an unwillingness to embrace harmony. If you are still active in irritating, opposing, hating, slandering, or sabotaging the other person, then peace is not possible. If you are going to be at peace, then you must stop all hostile actions and adapt to the melody of the other person's life and style. Every person is playing a melody with their life. They have a way they like to live. They have a rhythm and a style. Some people are more easily willing to change their tune and play your tune. Most, however, will not change until you have demonstrated a willingness to understand and adapt to their tune. If you are going to be in harmony with another person, then you must be willing to dance to their tune.

Many people have a secret cold war going on in various parts of their life. They have surrendered all openly hostilities, but they are not really trying to make peace. All this does is keep the tension going and eliminate the possibility of peace. What do I mean by a secret cold war? People will make snide or sarcastic comments about the other person. People will do something that they know frustrates the other person. People will adopt a bad attitude when they are around this other person. All of these forms of war are deniable but are really ways of saying, "I am not happy." "I want your life to be miserable." If you are going to have real peace you must stop all hostilities, even these "secret" wars.

Let me give you an example of what this looks like in business. If your company were bought out by another company, the new company would install their leadership and their way of doing business. You must decide whether you are going to be a part of the rebel alliance to keep the old ways alive or whether you will learn the new company's ways and join in whole-heartedly. This is not a matter of immorality or illegality, just familiarity. Will you be sarcastic or adaptive? Will you adjust to this new way or drag your feet because you liked the old way? If you get on board with the new company and truly make peace with them, then promotions, benefits, and raises are possible. If you continue a cold war for the old company that is gone, everybody is miserable.

The second aspect of real peace is harmony. If you were to really get along with this person, what would you have to do differently? If you were to "pretend" to enjoy this person, what would you have to be like? If you were to adapt to this person's personality, rhythms, interests, and needs, what would you have to do? It is active harmony that produces peace. I have watched as people have thrown themselves into enjoying this other person and they have discovered that they really do like the other person. Yes, they may have been rude. Yes, they may be different. Yes, they may have failed to treat you with the respect you deserve. But you will only learn whether you could be in a peaceful, enjoyable, harmonious relationship with this person by throwing yourself at adapting to them. Usually the other person will then be able to adapt to you.

There are a few people who are so self-focused that all they think about is themselves and how they want life to be. Let me clearly say that I am not suggesting you adapt to immoral, illegal, or unethical elements in the other person's life. If that is what another person demands, then it is permissible to move away from them and make peace through distance. But often the self-focused person can be won over to a peaceful respect of others through the techniques we will discuss in this section.

I have watched people avoid real harmony because they are afraid of what would be required: If I were to surrender to God, I would have to become a missionary and live in a thatched hut; if I were to really be in harmony with my wife, I would have to go to the opera or watch romantic movies every night; if I were to be in harmony with my husband, I would be wearing camouflage clothing and be in a boat fishing all the time. They have built up in their mind huge, uncomfortable, sacrificial actions that would be required if they were to really try and live with this other person in peace.

Making peace through understanding the tension in my life.

One of the first places to look for ways to make peace is to look at yourself. Galatians 6:7 *tells us that whatsoever a man sows that shall he also reap.* Therefore in some way what you are experiencing in terms of tension is because of choices you made or didn't make in that relationship. Let's take a look at the ten relationships in your life. Which areas in your life do you have tension? Most people report tension or difficulty in three of their major relationships at any one time.

God	
Self	
Marriage	
Family	
Work	
Friends	
Money	
Church	
Society	
Enemies	

Ask the Lord to reveal to you what ways you could have created or helped create the tension in that relationship. Harmony begins when you acknowledge to God and to yourself your part in creating the disharmony. You must ask yourself what it would look like to be in harmony with the right people. We can be in harmony with whomever we choose if we want to be in harmony.

Answer the following questions about the major relationships in your life where there is tension.

God: In what ways have you created the tension between God and you?

What would you have to do to live in harmony with God?

Self: In what ways have you created the tension between your ideal self and your actual self?

What would you have to do to live in harmony with yourself?

Marriage: In what ways have you created the tension between your spouse and yourself?

What would you have to do to live in harmony with your spouse?

Family: In what ways have you created the tension between your family and yourself?

What would you have to do to live in harmony with your family?

Work: In what ways have you created the tension between your co-workers, your bosses, and yourself?

What would you have to do to live in harmony with your co-workers and your boss?

Church: In what ways have you created the tension between your spiritual family and yourself?

What would you have to do to live in harmony with church leaders and fellow members?

Finances: In what ways have you created the tension in your financial life?

What would you have to do to live in harmony with your financial resources?

Friends: In what ways have you created the tension between yourself and your friends?

What would you have to do to live in harmony with your friends?

Society: In what ways have you created the tension between yourself and society?
>   (neighbors, city, government, police, IRS, INS, etc.)

What would you have to do to live in harmony with society?
>   (neighbors, city, government, police, IRS, INS, etc.)

Making Peace by Doing the Beatitudes

Let's look at each of the Beatitudes as ways to make peace. This overview exercise is designed to help you see whether your attainment of the qualities of the Beatitudes is high enough to inject peace into your relationships.

Ask God to tell you which of the Beatitudes you need more in your life to bring about harmony. Go through each Beatitude and pause, letting God speak about whether that Beatitude is the one that needs to be increased to bring about harmony in the relationships of your life: Poor in Spirit; Mourning; Meekness; Hunger and Thirst for Righteousness; Mercy; Purity of Heart; Peacemakers; Persecuted for Righteousness and for Christ.

1. Is it possible that I need to be poorer in spirit towards this person in order to reduce tension? Yes / No (humble, teachable, others-focused, aware of my strengths and weakness)

2. Is it possible that I need to mourn (process my pain, sins, losses) with this person in order to reduce tension? Yes / No (apologize, restitution, grieve, therapy, new perspectives)

3. Is it possible that I need to be meeker with this person in order to reduce tension? Yes / No (flexible, adaptable, calm, thoughtful requests, gentle)

4. Is it possible that I need to be more desirous of righteousness with this person in order to reduce tension? Yes / No (moral, cause-driven, strengths-focused)

5. Is it possible that I need to be more merciful with this person in order to reduce tension? Yes / No (gracious, merciful, beneficial, loving)

6. Is it possible that I need to be more pure in my heart with this person in order to reduce tension? Yes / No (focus on righteous goals, truth, positive, pure thought-life)

7. Is it possible that I can be more loving and/or harmonious with this person in order to reduce tension? Yes / No (love more, adapt at a new level, align more)

8a. Is it possible that I need to take a stand for righteousness in order to reduce tension? Yes / No (boundaries, willingness to suffer, dialogue)

8b. Is it possible that I need to take a stand for Christ in order to reduce tension with this person? Yes / No (clarity on worldview, willingness to suffer, dialogue)

I have found that often a change in one individual towards a more Christ-like demeanor will make all the difference in the other person being willing to be reasonable and in harmony. The more you act like Christ, the more they will be able to adapt to that level of love and joy. Yes, it is true that some will take advantage of Christ-like behavior. If this happens then God will prompt you when a stand for truth, righteousness, and God's glory is required.

Find out where the tension is coming from in the relationship

A number of years ago, in the midst of hundreds of hours of marriage counseling, I discovered what I came to call the relational grid. I discovered that there were only five major groups of problems in marriage. I would have couples understand those problems and work on the biblical solutions to the problems that they were experiencing. What I came to understand was that these problems were the same for every one of the ten major relationships in our lives. In other words, when one of the relationships of our life breaks down and has problems – whether it is our relationship with God, our children, our boss, our friends or our spouse – it all boils down to five problems. I have written extensively about these problems in relationship to marriage in my book *Marital Intelligence*, but the issues play out across all relationships in life.

1	2	3	4	5

Let me give you a quick overview of these places where the tension and difficulty can be coming from in your life. If we are to become deeply happy, then we must become peacemakers Jesus tells us. This means we have to understand how to create peace in our own life and in other people's lives.

Ignoring Needs	2	3	4	5

The first problem that relationships face is the problem of ignoring needs. Every relationship is in a sense a transaction. Both parties have needs and they expect the other person to meet their needs. If either party stops meeting the other person's needs, then there is a breakdown in the relationship. There are things that a boss expects an employee to do to keep their job. If the employee stops doing those things, then the relationship breaks down and the employee may get fired. There are things that the employee expects the boss to do. If the boss fails to do those things, then the employee may look for another job, start a union, become a whistleblower, or a hundred other things that say my needs are not being met. It is often easy to see at work; but it is not always easy to see that this is true in a marriage, it is true in a family, and it is true with our friends. Every relationship is built on both parties meeting the needs of the other party so that there is mutual appreciation of the relationship. Biblically this is called love. This means that it is important for each person in a relationship to learn what are the expectations and needs of the other person. Because if they are left undone, then the relationship breaks down.

1	Immature Behaviors	3	4	5

The second major problem is the problem of immature behavior. We would think that if an adult was having a problem in a relationship or having a personal problem, they would tell the other person and it would be sorted out. But people rarely do this. Most people resort to immature behaviors to signal that there is a problem. Immaturity seems to come in at least three different varieties.

The first is thoughtless immaturity. Thoughtless immaturity means you should have done something, but you forgot or neglected it because it was inconvenient. Almost everyone is involved with thoughtless immaturities on a regular basis. That is why we all need to be ready with an apology and an attempt to do better next time.

The second type of immaturity that wrecks relationships is intentional immaturity. This is where a person does something immature as a way of sending a signal that they are unhappy with the relationship. This is the husband who stays late at the office night after night in order to let his wife know he is not happy with something. This is the person who sarcastically makes a quip about something they wish they could really talk about. This is the colleague who intentionally messes up so that the other person will get in trouble. This is the teenager who pitches a fit in front of their parent's friends to let them know that things aren't okay with her.

The third form of immaturity is destructive immaturity. This type of immaturity is so toxic that just expressions of this level of immaturity can destroy a relationship. This is the person who goes and gets high or drunk because something in some relationship is not going right. This is the person who punches their spouse or girlfriend because they are losing an argument. This is the person who tries to rob a bank because money is tight, and they don't know what to do. This is the person who steals from the company to make ends meet or get back at what the company is doing to them.

1	2	Clashing Temperaments	4	5

The third major problem in relationships is clashing temperaments. This is a failure to accept people for who they are. All of us are attracted to those who are different from us, but then we often try and change them to be like us. If any relationship is really going to work, we are going to have to embrace the fact that every individual is different. These differences need to be understood and celebrated. If God put them in there, then they are not wrong but necessary. How can the relationship be adjusted to embrace this distinction? Too often people have a cookie-cutter approach to life. They believe that if people were more like them or fit a particular stereotypical mold, then everything would be okay. But whether it is a boss, a spouse, a child, or a friend, they are different from you. Their differences are not wrong (they can do immoral things and that is wrong), but the innate differences in the way they see the world and express who they are is not wrong.

1	2	3	Competing Relationships	5

The fourth major problem in relationships is competing relationships. We all have ten major relationships in our life and many times these fights with one another for time, energy, and resources. There is only so much time, and you only have so much energy and so many resources. You have to choose which relationship gets the most and which one gets the next amount of time and focus and so on down the line. It used to be true that everyone understood that love flowed out in a priority order. People used to realize that God was first, spouse was second, family was third, self was fourth, work was fifth to support the first four, and then the others lined up behind the first five. It seems that in our day and age all our relationships want to be in first place. This is an unrealistic arrangement to have all relationships competing for huge amounts of time, energy, and resources. It is imperative that we learn to give to all our relationships the right amount at the right time in the right way.

1	2	3	4	Past Baggage

The fifth major problem in relationships is past baggage. Everyone brings themselves into every one of their relationships. All of us have had things that have happened to us in the past that color who we are and twist our interactions. In many cases it is not until we process those past experiences that we can have a healthy relationship without the toxicity of the past damaging or even destroying the present.

There are three kinds of past baggage that crop up most often and need to be explored, so they do not sabotage your relationships. The first type of past baggage is victimization. If you (or your partner) have had significant abuse foisted upon you, then you must process that pain and oppression or it will leak out in a damaging way. I have worked with people who have suffered under the most awful forms of physical, sexual, verbal, and mental abuse. When they were willing to process their pain and the events that happened to them, it opened up a whole new world. Don't hide your past baggage. Find a safe person who you can share with and let them help you process that burden you have been carrying.

The second type of past baggage is family and cultural patterns. All of us were programmed to live life the way our parents and our culture lived life. In many cases this is wonderful. In other ways this is not helpful and can be destructive. We carry these damaging and destructive ways of living with us everywhere we go, and they hugely impact our relationships. Maybe we saw yelling and screaming modeled. Maybe we saw lying modeled. Maybe we had a ceiling of achievement put over our heads by the way our parents lived and the larger culture talked about us. Realize that you received good and bad things from your parents and culture, and these things should be processed as to whether they should remain in your behaviors and attitudes.

The third type of past baggage is past actions. This is where you did something that you knew was wrong. These past behaviors that are unprocessed and unforgiven twist a person. Realize that everyone has things that they did that they are not proud of and that need to be confessed and repented of so that forgiveness can flow into your soul. Do the work to make sure that your issues from the past have been dealt with.

If you are in a relationship and there is tension, then take a step back and examine the five problems and see where your tension is coming from and what can be done to fix it.

Ignoring Needs	Immature Behaviors	Clashing Temperaments	Competing Relationships	Past Baggage

8 Steps to Peace

One of the characteristics of Jesus Christ was that He brought peace to people so that they did not fight needlessly. We must be that same kind of person. There are a number of ways that we can be peacemakers.

Being at peace is like playing music with others. The instrument must be in tune, everybody must work with the same timing, each person must be in the right key, and everyone needs to know what the other person will be doing. These are the elements of harmony and beautiful music. These are also the elements of harmony and peace between people. Whether it is a marriage, a family, a business, a friendship or a church, harmony can be achieved and peace can be established when each person realizes that they are a part of a bigger whole. Each person has a part to play and those parts should be in harmony with all the other people.

Peace and harmony is destroyed when one person launches off on their own, playing their own melody without consulting with the others in the group. Peace and harmony is destroyed when one person is going faster or slower than everyone else.

Peace and harmony is destroyed when one person is out of sorts from some other part of their life and lets it impact the way they interact with this other part of their life. Peace and harmony are destroyed when one person lives out their assignments in a way that is completely different from the other people in the group. Whether you like it or not, you are in a group that needs your harmonies to create a beautiful life. It is not as simple as, "I would like to play my tune and have everybody else leave me alone." This won't work for you, and it won't work for the others in your group.

250

What are the tools or techniques of people who bring peace to a situation? The following is a list of eight exercises. Use at least one of these exercises to bring a new level of peace to others.

First, stop acting in an immature way. Sometimes there is a lack of peace because you have been acting in an immature or disrespectful way to others. If you stop and start treating everyone with respect, then there is a new level of peace. Treat everyone with a new level of respect and stop any immaturity.

In what ways are you acting immature in these relationships?

God	
Self	
Marriage	
Family	
Work	
Friends	
Money	
Church	
Society	
Enemies	

The first place to look for the solutions to peace is at yourself. Are you acting in an immature or selfish way that keeps this relationship in turmoil or hostility? Look at yourself.

Second, apologize for any problems, disrespect, or difficulties that you caused. Many times a simple apology for your part in a difficulty will open up the situation to being resolved. Even if you are only ten percent at fault and did not even cause the initial problem, apologize for your overreaction or your lack of respect. Your willingness to humble yourself will often work wonders.

In which relationships do you owe somebody an apology?

God	
Self	
Marriage	
Family	
Work	
Friends	
Money	
Church	
Society	
Enemies	

Practice apologizing, "I would like to apologize to you for hurting you. I realize my apology does not make up for the damage I caused, but I do hope you could forgive me."

Third, learn to align your expectations with other people before an event takes place. Ask the other people you are working with what they are expecting to happen this weekend or during this vacation. It is so helpful to understand ahead of time what the other person is expecting. If all the expectations are understood ahead of time, then these elements can be built in so that everyone is pleased.

In which relationships do you need to align your expectations?

God	
Self	
Marriage	
Family	
Work	
Friends	
Money	
Church	
Society	
Enemies	

Ask these people, "How can we align our expectations on this issue, event, topic?"

Fourth, make a thoughtful request for what you would like to see happen. Oftentimes there is a lack of peace because no one actually spells out exactly what they would like to have happen in a calm, thoughtful way. Our culture is often in love with the sarcastic, witty response that gets the laugh track going. This is not the way of peace.

What thoughtful requests do you need to make in each relationship?

God	
Self	
Marriage	
Family	
Work	
Friends	
Money	
Church	
Society	
Enemies	

I would like to ask if you could do this for me?

Fifth, add more love to the situation. Sometimes there is a lack of peace because there is a huge need that has not been met. To love is to meet needs. If there is a need that you can legitimately meet in the other person, then add that element of love. Some people have a hard time asking for their needs to be met. They just hope that someone will see it and meet it.

What are the dominant unmet needs in each relationship?

God	
Self	
Marriage	
Family	
Work	
Friends	
Money	
Church	
Society	
Enemies	

If I were to really meet your needs, what would I be doing that I am not currently doing?

Sixth, sometimes there can be no peace until a change is made in the other person. If that is the case, then that change must be addressed head-on and the needed changes must be started. This is never easy; but if the other person's change is absolutely required for peace, then that change must begin.

What are the key changes that the other person needs to make to make peace possible?

God	
Self	
Marriage	
Family	
Work	
Friends	
Money	
Church	
Society	
Enemies	

"Unfortunately, we cannot be at peace until this area changes." "I wish I did not have to bring this up but this issue has become so big that we are unable to have harmony in our relationship until it is resolved."

Seventh, clarify with the other person regarding the problem. Many people have a very difficult time having a hard conversation with someone who is damaging a relationship. "This has to stop because it makes me feel disrespected when you do it." A hard conversation spells out why there are problems, what should be done to resolve the situation, and when it should happen. In order to bring peace, there is a need for a clarifying conversation.

- I am hoping this is just a misunderstanding, but I remember... could you help me understand this in a different way?
- I could be wrong but I heard you (say or do) _____. Can you explain that to me because it causes me to take a step back in this relationship?
- I need to clarify something because right now I am very frustrated with you about... did this... really happen?
- I am struggling in this relationship because I understand that.... I cannot make peace with you until we get that cleared up.
- I need to clarify how hurt I am when you... I have a hard time seeing this relationship move forward until this behavior is stopped.
- I am hoping that I am wrong but I heard that you... and I need to know if that is true...
- Unfortunately, I have checked on... and I am being forced because of... to... (keep my distance, assign a repentance plan, fire you, not believe you, turn you in to the police, talk to a lawyer, wonder about your promotion) Now if there is something I am missing please let me know, but this... is a real killer of our relationship.

Eighth, requests for patience and a change of focus. Many times there is a lack of peace because one person has started to focus on the weaknesses and immaturities of another person. The offending person has lots of good qualities, but the focus is only on their inadequacies. If this focus on the negative is not stopped, there will be no peace. Start noticing all the positive in another person's life if you have been focusing on the negative. Ask for patience and shift your focus and peace will return.

Which relationships is God asking you to be patient and let Him work on the other person?

God	
Self	
Marriage	
Family	
Work	
Friends	
Money	
Church	
Society	
Enemies	

Secret #8

Persecuted for Christ and Righteousness

MATTHEW 5:11,12
*Blessed are those who have been persecuted
for the sake of righteousness
for theirs is the kingdom of heaven.
Blessed are you when men revile you and insult you
on account of me for so they persecuted the
prophets who were before you.*

8
Persecuted for Christ
and Righteousness

Setting Boundaries: Being different enough to be hated

One of the surprising qualities that Jesus tells us is needed for deep happiness is being persecuted. If we are going to truly be happy, then we must have moral and religious boundaries that we are willing to suffer for. Listen to the way Dr. Henry Cloud states this idea in his book *The Law of Happiness:*

"It's official. If you don't allow people to control you, abuse, you, or mistreat you, you will be happier. Research proves it, and the Bible tells us the same thing. But did we need scientists or God to tell us that?"

"The reason I say this is that people who suffer mistreatment at the hands of others often don't realize they are allowing it to happen. They don't realize how much control they could have over their own happiness if they would stop allowing themselves to be mistreated and affected by another person's behavior. In short they don't understand that they do not have good boundaries." (Henry Cloud, *The Law of Happiness*, page 135)

If you are going to be successful, happy, and/or blessed in life, you will have to start setting boundaries for yourself and for others. You have to say NO to yourself and to others to be blessed. In other words, you will have to begin placing limits on what you do and what you will allow others to do to you. In our day these are called boundaries. Make no mistake, when you start setting boundaries for yourself and others it will make others angry.

It is easier to always say YES, but there are behaviors that demand a NO. If we are going to obtain a higher level of God's blessing, we must begin limiting some of our options. Reaching maximum potential requires boundaries. You will have to say no to some things, some people, and some pleasures if you are going to be truly happy and/or blessed. Every Olympic athlete knows that they must give up some things in order to gain what they really want. These athletes give up certain kinds of food in order to maximize their bodies for competition. These athletes give up friendships that will get in the way of their training. These athletes give up certain activities that could distract them or damage them in their quest to gain Olympic gold. In the same way you will have to place limits on yourself and others. The Apostle Paul in 1 Corinthians 9:24-25 says the same thing, *Do you not know that those who run in a race all run, but only one receives the prize? Run in such a way that you may win. Everyone who competes in the games exercises self-control in all things. They then do it to receive a perishable wreath, but we are imperishable.*

Limits are essential for a happy life. That is why Jesus can say that you are blessed if you are ridiculed and even persecuted for having boundaries and limits. If you

261

have such a grip on righteous behavior that you won't let anyone push you into unrighteousness, you will move into a blessed zone. You have to see that blessings flow to the person who does not abuse and does not allow themselves to be abused. (I realize that some don't have a choice in their abuse and many do not realize that they have a way out). This whole book is designed to help people see their choices more clearly.

You and I are being manipulated if we have never said no to what others want us to do. In order to pursue God and protect yourself, you must set boundaries on what you do and what others can do to you. Not everyone will understand the boundaries that you are setting. Your boundaries will at times get in the way of what they want from you. As soon as you set boundaries for yourself and for others, you will begin to be persecuted, insulted, laughed at, pushed, reviled, and maybe even beat up physically. When you say that you won't let others use anger or violence as manipulative tools against you, they will push on that boundary to see if you will cave in. When you say that you won't allow yourself to be pushed into sexual unfaithfulness, you will be pushed on that issue. When you say that you won't put up with people verbally or emotionally abusing you, some will test your resolve; and then they will insult you, shun you and ridicule you if you do stand your ground. But think of these difficulties as preliminary evidence that you are on the road to a balanced and blessed life.

Let's do a thought exercise.

Is it possible for an employer to ask you to do so much for them that you no longer have a life outside of work?

262

Is it possible that a spouse or romantic partner could ask you to participate with them in activities that would trample on your moral boundaries or make you feel shamed or disrespected?

Is it possible for a child to ask you for permission to do something that would harm them or you?

Is it possible for a friend, colleague, or relative to ask you to be involved in something illegal, immoral, or dangerous?

The answer to these various situations is Yes and you must say No when anyone tries to push you out of the moral zone of blessing. You must have a personal ethic which limits your behavior and limits other people's behavior.

Now let's take this thought experiment a little further and explore the fact that some people will push you for their benefit and abuse you if they can. This is why you need personal boundaries. With the breakdown in Western culture of the Christian moral structure, abuse will grow. Everyone will be looking for how they can win, even if it requires that others lose in the process.

The Lord spelled out the truth of what we are supposed to do in the great commandments: *Thou shall love the Lord your God with all your heart, soul, mind, and strength and your neighbor as yourself*. This clearly states that the every-day goal of life is to love God, love yourself righteously, and love others. This positive goal is good, but it must have some clear negative definitions. What does it mean to not be loving? In almost every culture, love can be

263

defined as when I win and you lose. If my getting my way causes you to lose, then this is the evil. Only when you make sure that everyone wins (everyone is loved), can an action be called good. And when a person wins knowing that other people have to lose, this is evil.

This is the classic definition of good and evil. You can win but not if it directly results in a loss for someone else. This is what the Ten Commandments were given to spell out. Each of the Ten Commandments marked out a line where abuse would begin if you went too far. When a person steals, it means that someone else lost. When a person commits adultery, then this was a "win" for them but a loss for the spouse and families. When a person cursed and swore at someone, they felt like they won but the person who had to hear this verbal barrage lost. People lie for their own benefit and another person's loss. When an employer makes you work seven days a week and won't allow rest or worship, then they win and the employee loses.

Let me reintroduce you to the Ten Commandments. These limits on behavior are for the individual, but they are also for what others want to do to you. When God tells us, "Thou shalt not…" it is a limit on your behavior. But it is also a limit on other people's behavior to us. When we memorize and recite the commandments and say, "Thou shalt not…" it is for others who would try and force us into these destructive actions. I will show you the basic list of the Ten Commandments, and I also will write them out as affirmations of boundary limits.

Thou shalt not have any other gods before me
Thou shalt not make any graven images
Thou shalt not take the name of the Lord your God in vain
Remember the Sabbath Day to keep it Holy
Honor your Father and your Mother
Thou shalt not murder
Thou shalt not commit adultery
Thou shalt not steal
Thou shalt not bear false witness against thy neighbor
Thou shalt not covet anything that belongs to your neighbor
Are there any of these areas where you are living beyond the moral boundaries of the Ten Commandments?
Are you worshiping other gods?
Are you misrepresenting God with an idol?
Are you taking God's name in vain?
Are you remembering to rest and worship God at least one day a week?
Are you honoring your God-given authorities?
Are you using violence or the threat of violence to get your way?
Are you committing adultery?
Are you stealing?
Are you bearing false witness against your neighbor?
Are you coveting something that belongs to someone else?

Just as it is important to set limits on how much you eat and how much you spend, so it is important to set limits on your moral behavior. When you violate these commands, you are winning at someone else's expense. Stop and begin to live in the boundaries of righteousness.

Now, let me say that staying within the boundaries of the Ten Commandments does not make you perfect enough to go to heaven. That form of righteousness can only be supplied by God Himself. (which He has in the Lord Jesus Christ's life, death, and resurrection).

For some, you will need to enter into a process of bringing your life back in line with these moral strictures. There is great peace and joy inside these lines. There is deep happiness. There will be lots of people who will test you to see if you will keep to these new limits for yourself. It is worth it to maintain a moral lifestyle. Yes, some ways of getting rich and having fun are no longer available, but you will not be forcing a loss on others to "gain" for yourself. Life will go better.

Boundaries for others:

Not only do you need to put boundaries in place for yourself, you must put boundaries in place for how others treat you. People will abuse you if you are not clear on what behavior you will allow. Abuse is oppression and control of you through various means to provide a win for someone else at your expense. We live in a world where, increasingly, people are trying to take advantage of us for their own gain.

What are the most common forms of abuse?

Physical, Sexual, Verbal, Mental, Vocational, Emotional, Financial, Spiritual, Positional, Fraud.)

Let me give you a more complete understanding of these types of abuse.

Spiritual: The use of religion, God, or spiritual practices or ideas to oppress or control people. To force some form of loss on others through religion or spirituality to insure a gain for oneself.

Verbal: The use of words, names or labels to oppress or control. To force some form of loss on others through words, names, labels to insure a personal gain.

Emotional: Use of emotions to manipulate, oppress, or control. To force some form of loss on another through the use of emotions (anger, crying, love, shame, etc.) to insure another's personal gain.

Vocational: Use of financial or vocational needs to manipulate, oppress, or control. To force some form of loss on another through the use of finances to insure personal gain.

Positional: Use of position, power, or authority to manipulate, oppress, or control. To force some form of loss on another through the use of position, power, or authority to insure personal gain.

Physical: Use of violence or the threat of violence to manipulate, oppress, or control. To force some form of loss on another through the use of violence to insure personal gain.

Sexual: Use of sex to manipulate, oppress, or control. To force some form of loss on another through the use of sex and sexuality.

Financial: Use of stealing or defrauding to manipulate, oppress, or control. To force some form of loss on another through the use of stealing or defrauding to insure personal gain.

Manipulation: Use of lying, fraud, or half-truths to manipulate, oppress, or control. To force some form of loss on another through the use of lying, fraud, or half-truths to insure another's personal gain.

Mental: Use of scheming, inappropriate desire to manipulate, oppress, or control. To force some form of loss on another through the use of scheming, inappropriate desire to insure personal gain.

Everyone needs to be on guard against these forms of abuse. Let me remind you that we all live in a broken world where sin, evil, and selfishness exist. We must put ourselves, our loved ones, and others on constant reminder of these dangers or our lives will be sucked away serving evil or destroyed by it. The above lists the most common forms of abuse. God has powerfully helped us here in this matter of the basic boundaries for a sustainable happy life. If we put up his boundaries, they will protect us from most forms of abuse and the most destructive forms of temptation.

Remember, some of your best friends and even loved ones will try and sabotage your life by having you betray crucial limits and walk past essential boundaries. They will want what they want and God's boundaries will stand in their way. They will not care what happens to you after they have broken down your boundary. They will not be concerned that your life could spiral out of control or sink into depression or wander into destructive relationships. They will just want what they want when they want it. That is why you must protect your boundaries. You must not let these things happen. You have far more control than you realize. Yes, you will suffer various forms of persecution to protect yourself from these evils.

Below are the Ten Commandments restated as boundary markers for how you will allow others to treat you. This is how to say the Ten Commandments in our culture as we become increasingly lawless and permitting of win/lose scenarios.

1. I will not allow myself to be spiritually abused or manipulated

    No spiritual authority has the right to violate these boundaries

2. I will not allow God to be misrepresented to me

    No extra-biblical texts or secret knowledge that distorts the God of the Bible

3. I will not allow people to verbally abuse me or demean me

    No swearing, cursing, or demeaning me

4. I will not allow people to vocationally abuse me or deny my right to worship
   No excessive work or denial of worship

5. I will not allow people to use their authority or bitterness at authority to abuse me
   No absolute submission and no unwarranted rebellion

6. I will not allow myself to be emotionally or physically abused
   No leadership through anger or violence

7. I will not allow myself to be sexually abused
   No sexual unfaithfulness, exploitation, or harm

8. I will not allow myself to be financially abused or manipulated
   No stealing, tricking, or conning

9. I will not put up with people deceiving me for their own ends
   No lying, deceiving, fraud against me

10. I will not allow people to mentally abuse me
    No scheming against me – seeking to rob me of my personhood, possessions, or liberty

Now when we set up these boundaries, we must be prepared that people will want to break them down to get from us what they shouldn't have. In many cases upholding these boundaries means that we will need to walk away from a relationship with someone who won't respect our boundaries. Take this as a badge of courage that you are making progress. Not every behavior should be condoned. Some words do damage. Some impulses are destructive to you and to others. Some actions are good for the few but damaging to the many.

Jesus tells us that if we are going to truly be blessed, then we must begin setting boundaries for our behavior and for others' behavior in relationship to us. He plainly tells us that if we do not do this, then we will miss out on significant blessings, joy, and even happiness that could be ours if we did this. Let me help you understand this practically. Imagine a parent who wants his/her children to love them. They don't believe in restricting the child at all so there is never any limits on what the child can do, see, say, or act out. Does this child grow up to be successful or a wild child that will lie, hit, hurt, yell, and withdraw to get their way? We all know that a child must be taught to limit their natural impulses or they will harm others and their own potential. Parents must set boundaries for the children in all kinds of areas: when to go to sleep; what to wear; what to say and not say; where to go to the bathroom; what to eat; what to do with and to others.

Jesus actually puts the first half of the commandments after the second half of the commandments in this Beatitude. He talks about doing righteousness before He deals with our attitudes toward God and Himself.

What is the difference between setting boundaries and just being selfish? Some people demand that what they want takes place. That is being selfish. Jesus is not asking us to increase our selfishness.

271

Jesus tells us that we are to be salt and light in a dark world. Salt is a preservative of what is good and adds taste to meals. So we are to preserve what is good in the world and add flavor and taste to the world by our good works. Light is how we see. God wants us to be a part of the good in the world so that people will see our good works and glorify God. We can expect to be persecuted when we stand for the boundary lines in the Ten Commandments.

In what ways are you serving in the community to preserve righteousness or prevent unrighteousness?

Have you been persecuted for doing what is right?

Have you been insulted, mistreated, or persecuted for being a Christian?

If people were to look at your life, what good works are you doing that would cause them to glorify God for what you are doing?

Which of the Ten Commandments boundaries is most often neglected or trampled on in your community of friends and neighbors? How could you demonstrate the power and benefit of that moral boundary line?

Remember a good rule of thumb is two hours a week in the church, two hours a month in the community.

In what areas should you stand up for what is right?

Which of the Ten Commandments are being openly violated around you?

1. Thou shall have no other gods before me
2. Thou shall not make for yourself any graven images
3. Thou shall not take the name of the Lord your God in vain
4. Remember the Sabbath Day to keep it holy
5. Honor your Father and your Mother
6. You shall not murder
7. You shall not commit adultery
8. You shall not steal
9. You shall not bear false witness against your neighbor
10. You shall not covet anything that belongs to your neighbor

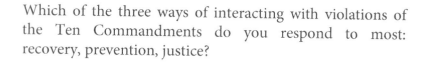

Which of the three ways of interacting with violations of the Ten Commandments do you respond to most: recovery, prevention, justice?

Recovery: Do you usually want to help people who are suffering under the consequences of violating the Ten Commandments?

Prevention: Do you usually want to help people so that they do not violate the Ten Commandments?

Justice: Do you usually want to stop perpetrators of oppression, abuse, and injustice?

Development: Do you usually want to help people reach their full potential and/or use all the talent, skills, and gifts that God has given them?

274

Conclusion

I became a follower of Jesus when I was seventeen. I was pointed at the Beatitudes as my goals. This is what Jesus said were the keys to a blessed life, so go after them. Various people have spoken into my life with exercises, projects, assignments, and information over the years. Every time I make progress on one of these qualities, my life improves in ways I could not have predicted. Every time I take a step back in one of these qualities, my life takes a step back to the selfishness, loneliness, and anger of my early life. I have truly been blessed in my life through the constant process of letting Jesus produce in me what He so clearly possessed. I have personally done all the exercises in this book and have counseled, mentored, and discipled hundreds of others in them as well. I can say without a doubt that Jesus was right. Gaining these qualities leads to a blessed life. I have been in the pursuit of these qualities for four decades, and I constantly discover new levels and new perspectives on the wonder of these qualities. I want to invite you into a lifelong pursuit to be like Jesus and enjoy the blessed life.

Remember that there will come times when God throws you a curve ball you were not expecting. He will do that because He sees more joy and more happiness that could come from your life than you are experiencing right now. He knows that you have no motivation to develop these Beatitudes that you desperately need. He knows that

He must bring you to embrace these qualities at new levels. He needs you to pass the quizzes, tests, and finals. He doesn't want you to settle for half of the deep happiness that is waiting for you. He knows that if you just had more humility, a new level of brokenness, a new ability to control your strengths and skills, more desire for righteousness, a willingness to let go of the wounds of others, more positive pure mental images, a greater ability to live in harmony with others, and/or a new willingness to suffer to for what is right, your life would take a leap to another level of joy. Don't miss these blessings grasping after money, popularity, or sensual pursuits.

Jesus says that keys to a blessed life are contained in these qualities. We would be very wise to pay attention. I have sought to give you multiple ways of developing these qualities, so that you will have a whole new level of deep happiness. Try the exercises in this book. Develop these qualities and drink in the blessing.

You can push away at these truths and refuse the wisdom contained in them. You could just push on with your own path to success, happiness, and joy. But that is what you have been doing, and we are beginning to see science confirm with astounding accuracy what Jesus gave us so clearly 2,000 years ago. I have included a few more exercises here in the conclusion so that you can drink in the depth and joy of the Beatitudes.

Exercise # 1

Pray and specifically thank God for each quality. Admit that you have resisted cooperating with His work in your life. Embrace what He is doing, asking for insight into how to learn the specific quality He is teaching.

1. Poor in Spirit - Are grateful, teachable, and humble

2. Mourning - Have processed your mistakes, wounds, pain, and losses

3. Meekness - Have developed impulse control and use your emotions to fuel and enjoy life

4. Desire for Righteousness - Pursue your dreams and righteous purposes with intensity

5. Merciful - Are forgiving, non-judgmental, and gracious

6. Pure in Heart - Think positive, beneficial thoughts rejecting unethical, depressive, and selfish thoughts

7. Peacemaker - Savor each day, harmonize with the people around you, and do not attack others

8. Persecuted for righteousness and for Christ - Set boundaries for yourself and others and are willing to sacrifice to protect those boundaries

Heavenly Father,

I come to you in the name of the Jesus Christ my Savior, and I want to thank you specifically for (one of the Beatitudes). I freely admit that I have, in the past, rejected this part of your plan for me. I now choose to accept_____ and to see your plan for me because of it. I am excited about the qualities of Christ that you will develop through this area. I believe that one of the things that you are doing with_____ is developing _____ in me, and I want to fully cooperate with the development of Christ-like qualities. Show me the ways that you want to use me through this "limitation" or haw you want me to conquer this "limitation" and expand my life message for you. Show me new ways to view this area of my life, that my perspective might become your perspective. Show me new insights from the Scriptures about how you used this area in others' lives to glorify you and to bring a new way of life to your servants. Today marks a new beginning. I will let your strength become perfect in my weakness. Open my eyes. I choose to thank you for _____ and to receive this as a mark to remind me of your power, grace, and love to deal with anything.

In the name of the Lord Jesus Christ,
Amen

Exercise #2

Think of the most significant irritation in your life right now. Pray until God makes it clear which qualities He is seeking to develop through this difficulty. I will often pray for God to show me which quality He has decided to work on in my life. I will let the needle float in my mind and let God show me.

Poor in Spirit

Mourning

Meekness

Hunger and Thirst
after
Righteousness

Mercy

Pure in Heart

Peacemakers

Persecuted for
Righteousness and
for Christ

Exercise #3

Pray the Beatitudes asking for God to develop in you these key qualities for a full and successful life. Write down what He says to you as you pray over each key quality. You may find yourself praying through this list often or once a year. As you grow as a person, you can look back at what you wrote down earlier as proof that you are making progress.

1. Poor in Spirit - Are grateful, teachable, and humble

2. Mourning - Have processed your mistakes, wounds, pain, and losses

3. Meekness - Have developed impulse control and use your emotions to fuel and enjoy life

4. Desire for Righteousness - Pursue your dreams and righteous purposes with intensity

5. Merciful - Are forgiving, non-judgmental, and gracious

6. Pure in Heart - Think positive, beneficial thoughts rejecting unethical, depressive, and selfish thoughts

7. Peacemaker - Savor each day, harmonize with the people around you, and do not attack others

8. Persecuted for righteousness and for Christ - Set boundaries for yourselves and others and are willing to sacrifice to protect those boundaries

Exercise # 4

Ask those who are closest to you and know you well, "Which of these qualities do I need most in my life?" "Which of these are limiting me more than others?" Make sure that you only ask those who are safe people who will not use this question as a chance to criticize or demean you. You do want them to be honest but not cruel.

1. Poor in Spirit - Are grateful, teachable, and humble

2. Mourning - Have processed your mistakes, wounds, pain, and losses

3. Meekness - Have developed impulse control and your emotions to fuel and enjoy life

4. Desire for Righteousness - Pursue your dreams and righteous purposes with intensity

5. Merciful - Are forgiving, non-judgmental, and gracious

6. Pure in Heart - Think positive, beneficial thoughts rejecting unethical, depressive, and selfish thoughts

7. Peacemaker - Savor each day, harmonize with the people around you, and do not attack others

8. Persecuted for righteousness and for Christ - Set boundaries for yourself and others and are willing to sacrifice to protect those boundaries

Exercise # 5

Affirm each day your embrace of the Beatitudes. "I want a blessed life" is what you are saying. When you choose to declare that you are going after a different kind of life, things begin to change. God says He can bless a life that is seeking relational wealth, not material wealth. He knows that it is only the life that knows how to develop real love and true wisdom that will ultimately succeed. The following is a paraphrased breakdown of the key ideas in the Beatitudes and speaking them out loud galvanizes these qualities as goals for your life. You will become alert to more opportunities to move in these directions as you say these affirmations each day. Read the statements out loud at least once a day for a week and see new choices you are alerted to and what begins to happen in your life.

- ✓ I am humble not needing to be the center of attention
- ✓ I am teachable, learning from everyone, learning every day
- ✓ I am grateful for all that God has given me
- ✓ I focus on my God-given talents, gifts, and abilities realizing I have weaknesses
- ✓ I take responsibility for my mistakes, wrongs, and errors
- ✓ I grieve my losses, processing and embracing them
- ✓ I am flexible, not demanding my own way
- ✓ I remain calm when others are emotional and reactive
- ✓ I make positive thoughtful requests and express my expectations wisely
- ✓ I act on my desire for the right and ethical in each situation
- ✓ I quickly forgive people's mistakes, wrongs, and attacks
- ✓ My soul nurtures kind, good, and loving thoughts and plans
- ✓ My words, thoughts, and actions bring about harmony everywhere I go
- ✓ I am willing to be insulted, wronged, and hated to stand for what is right
- ✓ I am a follower of Jesus Christ even if it brings insults and hatred

Exercise #6

Become familiar with the Beatitudes by writing, praying, typing, saying, and meditating on them. These are what God is trying to produce in your life so that you can have the best possible life. It would be very helpful if you were very familiar with the curriculum list from which God was choosing.

a. Write out the Beatitudes by hand, draw them, diagram them. There is something powerful that happens when we put the pen to paper and just write out these key qualities. It can also be very helpful to write them out in an artistic way.

b. Type out the Beatitudes and laminate them and say them in the shower as you are getting yourself ready for the day. Listen to God as you read out the Beatitudes. Is He saying that today you will focus on a particular quality? Is He warning you that you will need meekness or mercy today? These qualities are the language of a successful life from God's point of view; say them often.

c. Memorize the Beatitudes so that you are always ready to hear God answer the question "why?" If you say them every day, it will not be long before you have them memorized. Once you have them memorized, just let your mind flow in and around them throughout the day and let God speak to you about what He is doing in your life. He wants you to have these qualities more than you want to have them because they are the keys to a blessed life

d. Laminate the chart of the Beatitudes and their explanation for use as a placemat, shower reminder, bathroom mirror reminder, etc.

The Beatitudes	The happiest people...	I am sabotaging my life because I am still...
Blessed are the **Poor in Spirit** for theirs is the kingdom of heaven	1. Are grateful, teachable, and humble	1. self-focused, selfish, rebellious, and independent
Blessed are those who **Mourn** for they shall be comforted	2. Have processed their mistakes, wounds, pain, and losses	2. covering my mistakes, wounds, and pain with denial, silence, alcohol, drugs, pornography, sex, risk, etc
Blessed are the **Meek** for they shall inherit the earth	3. Have developed impulse control and use their emotions to fuel and enjoy life	3. full of anger, rebellion, and impulsiveness, using my strengths for what I want in the moment
Blessed are those who **hunger and thirst after righteousness** for they shall be satisfied	4. Pursue their dreams and righteous purposes with intensity	4. resistant to pursuing the dream God put in my heart and seeking pleasure without regard to who is damaged
Blessed are the **merciful** for they shall receive mercy	5. Are forgiving, non-judgmental, and gracious	5. harboring bitterness, judgmental, and plotting vengeance
Blessed are the **pure in heart** for they shall see God	6. Think positive, beneficial thoughts rejecting unethical, depressive, and selfish thoughts	6. filling my mind with sensuality, strife, vengeance, greed, and selfishness
Blessed are the **peacemakers** for they shall be called the sons of God	7. Savor each day, harmonize with the people around them, and do not attack others	7. fighting and attacking and do not want to adapt
Blessed are those who have been **persecuted for righteousness & Christ...** for theirs is the kingdom of heaven.	8. Set boundaries for themselves and others and are willing to sacrifice to protect those boundaries	8. putting up with abuse done to me and at times abuse others to get my way

Exercise #7

This test isolates / contrasts the Beatitudes with their opposite.

Would people you know tend to say you are…

Teachable	10 9 8 7 6 5 4 3 2 1	Set in your ways
Others-focused	10 9 8 7 6 5 4 3 2 1	Self-focused
Interdependent	10 9 8 7 6 5 4 3 2 1	Independent
Self-accepting	10 9 8 7 6 5 4 3 2 1	Self-loathing
Grateful	10 9 8 7 6 5 4 3 2 1	Ungrateful
Quick to apologize	10 9 8 7 6 5 4 3 2 1	Unapologetic
Processing pain	10 9 8 7 6 5 4 3 2 1	Stuffing pain
Angry	1 2 3 4 5 6 7 8 9 10	Calm
Flexible	10 9 8 7 6 5 4 3 2 1	Rigid
Adaptable	10 9 8 7 6 5 4 3 2 1	Inflexible
Rebellious	10 9 8 7 6 5 4 3 2 1	Team player
Driven	10 9 8 7 6 5 4 3 2 1	Unmotivated
Aimed right	10 9 8 7 6 5 4 3 2 1	Aimed at selfishness
Doing good	10 9 8 7 6 5 4 3 2 1	Doing harm
Filled with scripture	10 9 8 7 6 5 4 3 2 1	Filled with worldly ideas
Forgiving	10 9 8 7 6 5 4 3 2 1	Bitter
Vengeful	1 2 3 4 5 6 7 8 9 10	Merciful
Payback oriented	1 2 3 4 5 6 7 8 9 10	Let-it-go orientation
Ethical thought life	10 9 8 7 6 5 4 3 2 1	Immoral thought life
Thinking beneficial	10 9 8 7 6 5 4 3 2 1	Thinking selfish
Benefitting others	10 9 8 7 6 5 4 3 2 1	How do I get mine
Peace-maker	10 9 8 7 6 5 4 3 2 1	Peace-taker
Calm producer	10 9 8 7 6 5 4 3 2 1	Storm producer
Suffering for right	10 9 8 7 6 5 4 3 2 1	Protective of Self
Christ first	10 9 8 7 6 5 4 3 2 1	"Me" first
Mature faith	10 9 8 7 6 5 4 3 2 1	Immature faith
Boundaries	10 9 8 7 6 5 4 3 2 1	Few boundaries

How to Use this Book

Setting up a mentoring small group

These worksheets can be done by a person individually working through this book, but the maximum growth is usually achieved by gathering a small group of fellow believers who you can do this with.

Each session of the group should probably move through three phases.

Phase 1 when each member of the group tells what happened when they practiced the exercise the previous week. This may take ten to thirty minutes. It is important that every person in the group share. If someone in the group did not understand the exercise or did not do the exercise, then repeat the same exercise the next week. Do not move on just to get through the exercises. This is not about moving through the material. It is about the material moving through you.

Phase 2 is where the leader explains the next week's exercises with a demonstration. The explanation is not a study; it is a simple explanation of how to do the exercise. There should be an explanation of what Scripture the exercise is based upon.

Phase 3 involves taking one prayer request from each member of the group. If a participant does not have a personal prayer request, then the other members are to pray whatever God brings to mind when they think of them. The whole meeting should take an hour to an hour and a half. I will often do this over breakfast or lunch.

Sometimes this material is a part of a class at church with more than five people. If your group is larger than five, then subdivide the group into multiple small groups of three people. In class settings the temptation is to have the second phase go longer than twenty minutes. Resist that temptation. Remember, you are explaining a spiritual exercise so that people can do it, not teaching the deep nuances of God or spiritual exercises.

I have included many exercises in each chapter so that you, as an individual, or the group could spend a number of weeks working on a particular quality if that is the one that God is directing you towards. Some people have focused on one quality for months, skipping the other qualities until they need those exercises.

Supplemental material is recommended throughout this book that will give a deeper explanation and greater detail on the specific spiritual and/or relational exercise that is being recommended.

Bibliography

Shawn Anchor, *The Happiness Advantage*, Crown Publishing Group, a division of Random House, Inc., New York, NY

Henry Cloud, *The Law of Happiness: How Spiritual Wisdom and Modern Science Can Change Your Life (The Secret Things of God)*, Howard Books, a division of Simon & Schuster, Inc., New York, NY

Gil Stieglitz, *Marital Intelligence: A foolproof guide to saving and strengthening your marriage*. BMH books, Winona Lake, Indiana.

Gil Stieglitz, *Spiritual Disciplines of a C.H.R.I.S.T.I.A.N.* Principles to Live By, Roseville, CA. 2005 Third Printing

Gil Stieglitz, *They Laughed When I Wrote Another Book On Prayer*. Principles to Live by, Roseville CA. 2010

Gil Stieglitz, *Touching the Face of God*. Principles to Live By, Roseville, CA. 2010.

About The Author

Gil Stieglitz is an internationally recognized author, speaker, catalyst, counselor, professor, and leadership consultant. He is Executive Pastor of Adventure Christian Church, a mega-church of 4,000 in Roseville, California. He teaches at Christian Universities and graduate schools in practical theology (Biola, William Jessup, Western Seminary). He is the President of Principles to Live By, an organization committed to teaching God's principles in a life-giving way. He sits on several boards, including Thriving Churches International, a ministry extension of Bayside Church, and Courage Worldwide, an organization that builds homes throughout the world to rescue children forced into sexual slavery. He has been a denominational executive for fifteen years with the Evangelical Free Church of America and was the senior pastor of a vibrant church in southern California for seventeen years.

Other Resources by Gil Stieglitz

BOOKS
Becoming Courageous
Breaking Satanic Bondage
Developing a Christian Worldview: Intensive Training in
  Christian Spirituality
God's Radical Plan for Husbands
God's Radical Plan for Wives
Going Deep In Prayer: 40 Days of In-Depth Prayer
Leading a Thriving Ministry: 10 Indispensable Leadership Skills
Marital Intelligence: A Foolproof Guide for Saving and
  Strengthening Marriage
Mission Possible: Winning the Battle Over Temptation
Spiritual Disciplines of a C.H.R.I.S.T.I.A.N.: Intensive Training
  in Christian Spirituality
They Laughed When I Wrote Another Book About Prayer,
  Then They Read It: How To Make Prayer Work
Touching the Face of God: 40 Days of Adoring God
Why There Has to Be a Hell

PODCASTS
Becoming a Godly Parent
Biblical Meditation: The Keys to Transformation
Everyday Spiritual Warfare
God's Guide to Handling Money
The 4 Keys to a Great Family
The Ten Commandments

If you would be interested in having Gil Stieglitz
speak to your group, you can contact him through the website
www.ptlb.com